The Proper Care of
DISCUS

Title page: A beautifully planted Discus show tank is well within the reach of the motivated hobbyist.

Photographs and Illustrations: Aqualogics, Dr. Herbert R. Axelrod, P. Barker, C. Barrell, Dr. C. Chan, K.L. Chew, D. Cooley, B. Degen, I. Francais, H.-J. Franke, Dr. R. Geisler, M. Gilroy, U. Glaser, Dr. H. Grier, D. Jordan, B. Kahl, H. Linke, C.O. Masters, H. Mayland, F. Mohlmann, F. Mori, H. Musstopf, A. van den Nieuwenhuizen, J. Palicka, J. Quinn, K. Rataj, H. J. Richter, F. Rosenzweig, D. Schlingmann, V. Serbin, F. Siedel, H. Stolz, D. Untergasser, Bede Verlag, J. Wattley, H. Yamada, Lo Wing Yat, R. Zukal

The Proper Care of
DISCUS

BERND DEGEN

CONTENTS

Foreword
Introduction to a Fine Hobby 11
The Discus Show Tank 33
Water for Discus 69
Stocking Your Show Tank 111
Foods and Feeding 151
Breeding Discus 179
Suggested Reading 254
Index 255

Bernd Degen, the author, has a great love of Discus.

Foreword

Before you is a completely new book with the title *The Proper Care of Discus*. The contents of the book ought to do justice to the title. Therefore, in this book you will find many suggestions which will ultimately bring you success with your Discus. I wrote this book from my rich store of experience acquired in the course of years of caring for and breeding the "King of the Aquarium." I have worked intensively with Discus for a good twenty years. I have observed again and again that new situations suddenly developed in the care of these fish. Again and again I gained new knowledge and added to that knowledge. Because of my numerous contacts with Discus fanciers

Young turquoise Discus with high bodies, large dorsal and anal fins, and excellent pelvic fins.

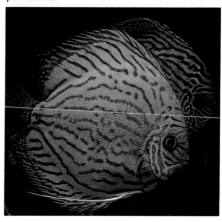

throughout the world, I feel confident in saying that I have great insight into the Discus scene. At every visit to a Discus fancier, whether it was in a large breeding installation in Asia or in a small hobbyist's cellar in Germany, I saw something interesting, which I would like to share with you in this book. This book primarily deals with the successful care and breeding of Discus. It contains my personal experiences—those with which I have been successful. For that reason it could by all means happen that these observations will differ from standard opinion, and that some details will not agree with those found in my other Discus books. It is really intended to be that way. This book is meant to be a kind of "cookbook" for Discus fanciers. You really can begin the individual steps with, "Take . . ."

I wish you much pleasure in the study of this book and a lot of fun with your hobby.

Bernd Degen

Facing page: A small shoal of wild brown Discus looking very contented in their well-planted aquarium.

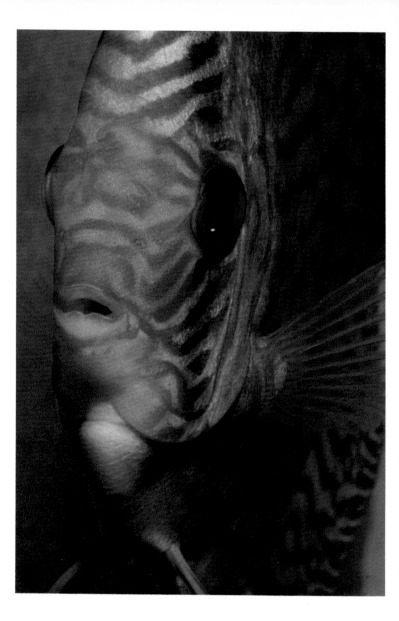

Introduction to a Fine Hobby

The aquarium hobby with all its variations is a very old hobby. The aquarium owner very quickly develops a close relationship with his or her fishes. This is particularly true with larger fishes. It is understandable that it is not possible to have as intimate a relationship with a school of Neon Tetras as with a pair of Discus. This, however, is not based solely on the size of the Discus, but on their behavior too. Discus are cichlids, and

Facing page: There are few things more thrilling to the Discus fancier than the trusting gaze of a well-kept Discus.

this family of fishes is known for its interesting behavior in the aquarium. No other fish family is as popular with hobbyists as the cichlid family. Large cichlids know and learn to recognize their keeper. This may sound somewhat strange, but hobbyists who have kept Discus for a while can confirm it. The Discus soon learns to recognize its keeper and greet him when he approaches the aquarium. The fish also soon learns when and how it will be fed. The fish swims automatically to the feeding place which is familiar to it through the daily feedings. Accordingly, it can be established that Discus can very quickly learn a procedure. The main attraction of these fishes is doubtless the unique brood care they carry out in rearing their young. Discus rear their fry for a period of several weeks. In so doing they feed the fry with a skin secretion containing large numbers of bacteria that stimulate the vital digestive functions of the fry. The nourishment of fry with rearing food produced by the parents' bodies is rare in fishes. This complicated brood behavior also makes the breeding of Discus particularly difficult. Yet, people are fascinated by difficult tasks. This is doubtless one reason why Discus breeding can be considered the crowning achievement in the freshwater aquarium hobby. Every serious hobbyist probably has toyed at some time with the idea of keeping and breeding Discus.

Discus certainly are not much harder to keep than other aquarium fishes. In a community tank with Neon Tetras, Guppies, Angelfish, and other fishes, a fish will die from time to time. Because they are "cheap fishes," however, it scarcely merits discussion. When a

Facing page: Even very young Discus recognize their keeper. Like with puppies, early socialization plays an important role in the temperament of the adult Discus.

When you have this many adult Discus in an aquarium, you have a considerable emotional investment, not to mention any other considerations.

Discus becomes ill and dies, however, an expensive fish that the hobbyist has grown fond of will have perished. This loss will be harder to get over.

When fishes die for some reason in the community tank, this will hardly be grounds for getting rid of the aquarium. But if several Discus die one after the other, the Discus fancier will soon have doubts and may even give up the hobby. This does not have to be the case, however, as long as basic rules in the care of Discus are followed.

Dr. Herbert R. Axelrod and Bernd Degen examine Bernd's breeding stock. Notice how eager the fish are to see what's going on when Dr. Axelrod puts his hand to the glass!

The original wild-type
Discus were collected in
the Amazon basin and
currently there are several
subspecies. These wild
Symphysodon discus
discus *are one such
subspecies.*

A show tank like this cannot be achieved overnight. This beautiful display is the result of knowledge, careful planning, attention to detail, and most importantly, the labor of love.

NATURAL REQUIREMENTS

Discus come from the Amazon Basin of South America, where they are found in a number of rivers. The average temperature of the water in which Discus live is 86°F. The pH is in the slightly acid range, and in the so-called

The native waters of the Discus. Discus are commonly found where there is lots of cover in the form of tangled roots from the trees at water's edge.

Discus in the wild are elusive. They hide well. The intrepid explorers who discover new Discus forms are to be commended for their curiosity and dedication.

blackwater rivers where the Heckel Discus lives, the pH can even be less than 4.0. The electrical conductivity of the water is very low and is often less than 10 microSiemens. Logically, these extreme values must be taken into account in the aquarium. Typical Discus waters also hold very few aquatic plants because this water cannot be described as exactly favorable for plant growth.

These natural requirements for successful Discus keeping are not easy to reproduce in the home aquarium. Water quality is highly variable. Each town or district has its own type of water. In some cases, for example, only very hard tap water is available. This hard water must be softened and prepared. Hobbyists who have the good fortune to live in a part of the country with very soft water can dispense with extravagant water preparation media. As far as possible, wild-caught Discus should be kept in aquarium water that approximates the water found in their natural conditions. Time and again the water for Discus is too cold. The conductivity presents fewer problems than does the proper pH for keeping Discus. The pH should not be higher than the neutral point of 7.0. But the other extreme—a pH of less than 4.5—also must be avoided under any circumstances. A constant pH of about 6.0 to 6.5 is ideal. This range corresponds to the values found in most river systems in the Amazon.

The quiet, serene waters that are home to the Discus are also soft, acidic and warm. These are the conditions that must be recreated in the aquarium!

A Discus aquarium can of course have a substrate. This also corresponds to the

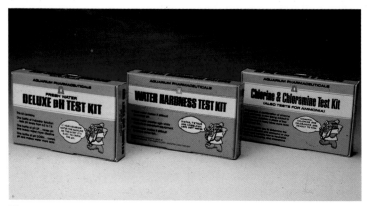

The correct water conditions are critical to the health and vigor of your Discus. Fortunately, test kits are easy to use and inexpensive. There is no excuse for neglect in this area.

natural living space of these fishes. Nevertheless, the substrate should not be too coarse, because Discus like to blow into the substrate in search of food. A sandy substrate with a grain size of 2 to 3 millimeters is ideal. A bare aquarium is preferable for spawning, because it is easier to control and clean. Roots and plants can also be introduced into a Discus aquarium. In the selection of the plants, make sure they can tolerate the fairly high temperatures of the Discus aquarium. The roots must not release any moldy odors into the aquarium or foul the water unnecessarily. An aquarium for Discus furnished in this manner can certainly meet the natural requirements of Discus. Every hobbyist knows by now that a large aquarium is considerably easier to care for than a small aquarium, so the final advice in this section is that it is better to buy an aquarium that is a little too large than one that is too small.

WATER PREPARATION AND TREATMENT

Water is the element of life for our Discus. Most Discus fanciers only have access to pure tap water. This tap water is usually

Wild brown Discus grace a well-planted aquarium. The wild stock is necessary to infuse vigor into the domestically developed strains.

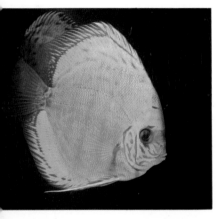

adequate for keeping Discus, particularly if it is not too hard.

The total hardness of the water is measured in German degrees of hardness (DH). Total hardness is defined as the sum of all of the so-called "earth-alkali" ions dissolved in water. The principal ions here are calcium and magnesium. At about 80 percent, they make up the largest percentage of cations. Calcium is essential for fishes for building their skeletons. Magnesium, on the other hand, is required by Discus only as a trace element. Magnesium influences bodily processes. More important than

Top: German "Wattley" type.
Center: Cobalt blue turquoise.
Bottom: Cobalt blue turquoise.

hardness for Discus, however, is the conductivity of the water. Conductivity measures the flow of electric current in water. The higher the concentration of ions, the better the current is conducted. For example, salt water has a very good conductivity, and surges of electricity can be far more dangerous in salt water than in fresh water. Water with one degree of German hardness has an average conductivity of 33 microSiemens per centimeter. This average value can serve as a reference point.

The water in the Amazon region mostly

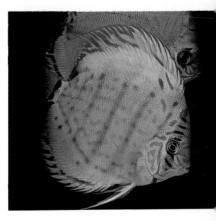

Top: Cobalt blue turquoise. **Center:** Cobalt blue turquoise. **Bottom:** Cobalt blue turquoise.

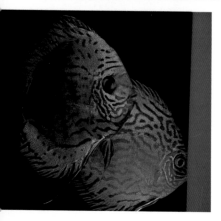

Top left: *Adult male German "Wattley" turquoise. Turquoise Discus have a tendency to require more stringent attention to environmental conditions.*
Top right: *Cobalt blue Discus. This pattern of stripes is common in the cobalt blue Discus.*

has a very low conductivity. It is often less than 10 microSiemens because it contains almost no carbonate hardness. In the blackwater region of the Rio Negro the pH is less than 4.0 and the conductivity is much less than 10 microSiemens. This water has a very high concentration of humic acids, which in turn ensures a low pH. The humic acids are created by the incomplete decomposition of plants, which is the same mechanism responsible for peat formation. These humic and fulvous acids give the Discus water its unique black-water character. Most Discus, however, do not live in pronounced black water, but in mixed water with a pH of more than 6.0. Even this water has a very low electrical conductivity, however.

So we need soft water for our Discus, particularly for breeding. Discus that have been bred over several generations in the aquarium also easily tolerate water with a fairly high conductivity and total hardness. Hobbyists report again and again that they have bred Discus successfully in fairly hard water. This leads to the conclusion that the electrical conductivity or the total

Discus may breed in hard water, but why try to thwart them? For large, healthy spawns, provide their preferred water conditions.

This fantasy tank is not an accident. Chemically stable water and adequate lighting have created a balance that enhances the lives of both fish and plants.

hardness are not necessarily decisive for breeding Discus successfully. Trace elements usually play a bigger role than the abundant elements such as calcium or magnesium.

A significant advantage of harder water with higher conductivity is the greater stability as regards pH. Harder water has a far more even pH and is not prone to sudden fluctuations.

On the other hand, fairly soft water continues to be necessary for breeding Discus. Successful breeding is of course also possible in harder water, but breeding success of this kind could be positively influenced by completely different factors. Thus, there is no such thing as the perfect water for spawning Discus. The conductivity and the total salt content of the water determine its osmotic pressure.

In osmosis, water molecules pass through a semipermeable partition. Osmosis can perhaps be explained best using the example of a Discus egg. There is an osmotic pressure inside the Discus egg, and an osmotic pressure likewise prevails in the water surrounding the egg. If the osmotic pressure inside and outside the egg is about equal, the membrane of the egg

Discus eggs have a hard time hatching into Discus fry when they are laid in hard water.

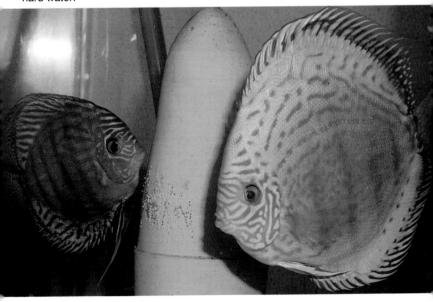

Neon Tetras also require soft water for successful hatching of the spawns.

will not be damaged. If there is a large pressure difference, however, the membrane of the Discus egg will be destroyed by this pressure gradient. This is often the reason for the failure of Discus breeding.

The osmotic pressure gradient between the egg and the environment causes the egg either to shrivel or swell. Most of the eggs can survive and adapt to small osmotic fluctuations or changes without damage. Nonetheless, the Discus eggs and the spermatozoa that will fertilize them have a hard time surviving in hard water, and for this reason the breeding of fishes from typical soft-water regions is often unsuccessful in the aquarium. A typical example here is the Neon Tetra. It can be bred successfully only in extremely soft water. Because the osmotic pressure of water depends on its total hardness, most of the calcium hardness should ideally be removed for breeding Discus. Two completely different systems are suitable for lowering water hardness: first, ion exchange, and second, reverse osmosis. The principles and equipment required for ion exchange and reverse osmosis will be discussed in further detail in the chapter "Water for Discus."

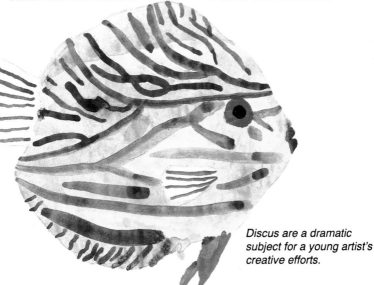

Discus are a dramatic subject for a young artist's creative efforts.

The Discus Show Tank

Discus are often kept or bred in sterile, unfurnished aquaria. This has given them the reputation of being very delicate, difficult fish that require constant tending and supervision. This supervision and regular water changes have no doubt led to their being kept in this way by the professional Discus breeder. However, *any* professional fish breeder, of Angelfish or Guppies or Discus, is going to keep his fish in the barest possible aquarium because, let's face it, commercial breeding is a different ball game. The commercial breeder is not into the aesthetics of the aquarium; beauty to him is a 100% hatch rate, sterile, bare aquaria, and brimming vats of brine shrimp nauplii.

An attractively planted aquarium with a school of serene, healthy Discus and even other species of compatible fishes need not be a hobbyist's unfulfilled pipe dream. On the contrary, if you are primarily interested in keeping Discus

Facing page: This lavishly planted aquarium is interesting to look at and one can only conclude that it is a comfortable home for the Discus as well.

While plastic plants and blue gravel may not be to everyone's taste, the fish don't seem to mind as long as their other needs are met.

rather than breeding them, it is best to keep them in a fully furnished, homey aquarium. You will soon see that a decorated Discus show tank is little more work and certainly much more pleasure than a sterile keeping tank.

THE AQUARIUM

For a Discus show tank, the aquarium *must* be large enough. It certainly makes no sense to start this kind of undertaking in a 20-gallon tank. A minimum size of 50 gallons is recommended. There are of course no upward

There is a philosophical attitude among most experienced aquarists that compels them to choose natural themes for their aquaria.

This strongly colored blue fish shows a lot of red because of good aquarium lighting.

limits and so the ideal show tank for you might be 125 gallons. The aquarium for Discus should be proportionate in size to the number of fishes you intend to keep. If you are interested in keeping only a breeding pair, then a 30-gallon tank will suffice. If you want a busy community tank, think in the range of 50 to 100 gallons.

The tank itself should be the standard rectangle. The fancier

Larger tanks are always good investments. If you buy a small one now, you will just want a bigger one later.

A good, deep tank gives Discus ample room to develop normally.
There is also less chance that they will concuss themselves on the
glass if they should take fright and dash madly around the tank.

shapes like hexagons and cylinders just won't give you the surface area you need for proper water quality. Also, Discus need height in the aquarium. Their shape mandates that they have a high enough tank to be comfortable.

The aquarium can be either glass or acrylic.

It's strictly a matter of personal preference. Most important are size, shape, and quality. Considering the value of the fish you intend to keep, quality becomes especially important. Never buy a repaired leaker or a used tank, or a discount-store tank. Only buy a well-known brand name

These perfectly matched Discus are a credit to their keeper.

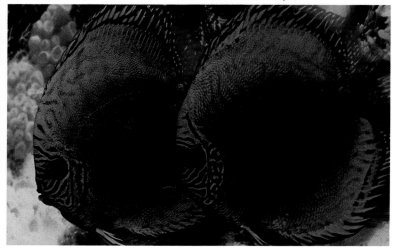

from a reputable pet shop. The dealer who sells Discus will fully understand the necessity of a quality tank and will provide the same. When purchasing an all-glass aquarium, make sure that it is not chipped, and that the edges are nicely beveled so that they will not cut you when the aquarium is handled.

The larger the tank is, the thicker the glass must be to withstand the tremendous pressure water can exert. Very big tanks will have center supporting struts fitted on top from front to back. All quality tanks will feature supports for a glass cover; highly recommended for limiting the amount of dust that will fall onto the water's surface, and to minimize water loss through evaporation. Glass covers for large tanks should be hinged for access without having to remove the cover.

THE BACKGROUND

The rear and side glass of the aquarium naturally should be covered. Various attractive backgrounds are available from your pet dealer. Another possibility is to paint the outside of the aquarium with waterproof paint. Synthetic enamel has proven to be a good choice. Do not choose a dark color; a light one is better. From experience it can be said that light green or light brown are

These are not your traditional aquaria, but they satisfy all the needs of the Discus they house. They certainly add a touch of class to the establishment.

optimal. It's really a matter of taste—yours and the Discus. However, the Discus show no fright reaction at all in aquaria with these kinds of backgrounds.

Discus are accustomed to receiving their light from above, and in the confines of the aquarium can be very nervous about light that comes from other directions. Since fish are phototrophic (they lean towards the light), it is not inconceivable that if your Discus aquarium received substantial light from one side that the fish would eventually swim at an angle.

The insides of the rear and side glass can also be covered with a suitable decorative material; for example, pieces of slate can certainly be layered in the background or sheets of cork glued on. Decorative materials installed in the aquarium, however, must be tested for possible toxicity. It is best to stick with known commodities when putting anything into your aquarium. Any good pet shop will offer a vast array of *safe* decorative items for the aquarium.

THE SUBSTRATE

Another important factor for the well-being of Discus is the right substrate for the aquarium. A two-inch

Facing page: This giant red turquoise shows up well even in its bare tank thanks to the decorative aquarium background.

layer of sand is always appropriate. Fine, round gravel can also be used. The diameter of the gravel must not be more than 2 to 3 millimeters, however. Discus are bottom feeders and if the gravel is too coarse a lot of food will disappear into the substrate, where it will soon start to decompose.

Discus like a sandy bottom best, because they can blow into it to look for food. Watch how a Discus glides over the bottom, tilts its head down, and carefully blows into the sand. If it has swirled up food in this manner, it can grab and swallow it quickly. Sharp-edged or pointed gravel is completely unsuitable as a substrate. The fish can easily injure themselves on it. The very popular pumice is also unsuitable for Discus because of its sharp edges.

The substrate must be rinsed very thoroughly before it is put in the aquarium. This is best done with lukewarm water. The rinsed substrate is poured into the aquarium and spread uniformly over the bottom.

DRIFTWOOD AND ROCKS

Now decorative elements, like rocks or roots, are added. Roots that start to rot in water must never be used. Special xyloliths or savannah roots, which are particularly suitable for the aquarium hobby,

The substrate preferred by Discus is fortunately ideal for plant growth.

are commercially available. These must not have sharp edges. In addition, they should not leach hardening elements into the water. Calcareous sandstone, for example, is not

You can be as generous as you wish in your use of plants, driftwood, and rocks in your show tank.

suitable because it hardens water.

Rocks do, however, add interest to a show tank. There is no reason not to use decorative and functional rocks in a Discus show tank. Often Discus will spawn on an attractive piece of upright slate. They are also useful for anchoring the roots of wandering greenery. While the world is full of rocks free for the taking, do yourself and your fishes a favor and stick to safe rocks available at your pet shop. Unless you are absolutely certain the rocks you find in your backyard are not going to leach toxins or calcium into the water, the pet shop rocks are far cheaper when compared to the cost (and heartbreak) of replacing a tankful of fishes.

Electronic submersible heaters easily and accurately preset to your desired temperature.

HEATING

Discus have evolved to live within a certain temperature range. The temperature in the Amazon and its tributaries is fairly constant at around 86°F. All fishes suffer if subjected to water hotter or colder than that in which they have genetically evolved to live, and, regardless of their relative hardiness, all fishes will especially suffer if the temperature changes more than 35°F within a

Submersible heaters usually attach to the sides of the tank with suction cups.

Japanese strain of high-fin turquoise morphs.

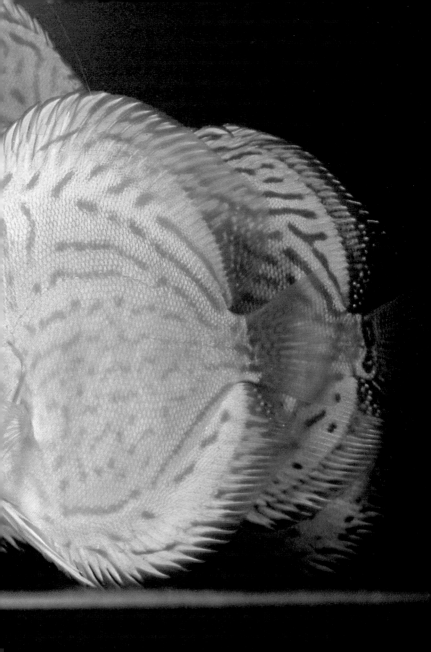

12-hour period. Although a sudden rise in temperature is more easily tolerated than a sudden drop of the same dimension, temperature changes upward create an additional hazard because as the water heats up, it is less able to hold oxygen. In a heavily stocked aquarium this might prove to be fatal to the fishes. As the temperature rises so does the activity level of the fishes, thus when combined with a reduced oxygen level, it can be seen just how important it is to provide the preferred temperature for Discus.

It may be possible to keep Discus without additional heat in warm climates, but if the overnight temperature drops, it is possible that the fishes will become ill or even die, so even in warm climates it is advisable to have a heater in the tank to prevent catastrophic drops in temperature.

There are many heaters on the market, but the most popular type these days is the submersible heater controlled by a thermostat. Preset submersible heaters can be calibrated to the desired temperature and will ever after maintain that temperature.

With the clip-on heaters the temperature can be adjusted

Facing page: A very attractive Discus color morph called Red Dragon in the trade.

externally but these models are not usually as reliable (or as costly) as the fully submersible units. The latter, however, have the disadvantage that when adjustments are needed the heater must be unplugged and allowed to cool down for a few minutes, as it must be removed from the aquarium in order to make the adjustments.

Clip-on heaters are not waterproof so must never be fully submerged.

Heaters should never be placed into the gravel; this can result in uneven heating of the glass casing, which might then shatter, or at least crack and allow water to enter the heater with dire results. The heater can be placed into a plastic sheath that is perforated with holes. This will prevent fishes from accidentally rubbing themselves against the heater, which might burn them, depending on the power of the unit.

In large aquaria it is always better to use two heaters, one at each end of the aquarium, than one high-wattage heater. This not only ensures more even distribution of heat, but if one heater fails then at least the temperature drop will take much longer, as it is unlikely both will fail at the same time.

The heater should be placed so that it heats the lower levels, thus creating an upward current of warm water.

The heaters can also be placed into some of the external filters, thus forming a thermofilter, but here the problem is that if the filter fails for any reason then the heating system is out as well.

Space heating is sometimes used by people who have a separate "fish room" and a large number of tanks. The idea is that it is cheaper to heat a room to a given temperature, and thus all aquaria in it, than to heat the tanks individually. It is a system that is only worthwhile if you have many tanks. Even so, this system has its flaws. The temperature must be slightly higher than required by the fishes to ensure that the

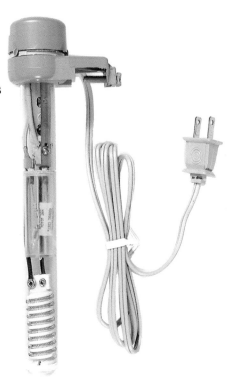

Clip-on type heaters must never be submerged below the water line mark on the glass casing.

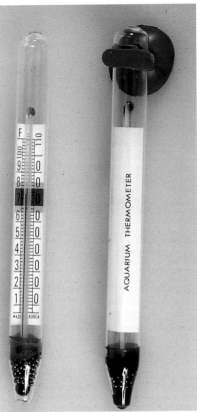

Water temperature is very important to the health of your Discus. Don't forget the simplest accessory, your thermometer.

water temperature is high enough, and many times the lower level tanks are chilly, while the upper level tanks are on the warm side. Water temperature aside, most of us find it difficult to spend any amount of time in a room that is humid and over 85°F.

Even though the heater may be controlled by a thermostat, you should always use an internal or external thermometer, or both, for the aquarium. A thermostat may fail, and this can result in the water temperature rising to the full potential of the heater. This may just be enough to cook the fish! On the other hand, it might jam in the closed position so the heater does not come on. The thermometer is thus a very valuable, yet inexpensive, accessory.

There are numerous types of thermometers available, each having their own advocates. Some are free-floating, some are standing, others are fixed inside the tank with suction cups, and yet others can be clipped to the side of the aquarium. The newest types are liquid crystal and can be attached to the outside of the tank in a convenient, yet unobtrusive place. They are self-adhesive and very accurate. Do not use a mercury thermometer inside an aquarium; should it break the poisonous contents will kill the fishes. Alcohol is a much better fluid for inside models.

LIGHTING

That Discus must be kept in semidarkness is an old wive's tale, which, however, has remained entrenched in the literature. An aquarium occupied by Discus can be lit completely normally without further ceremony. Light is a

Yes, Discus are often photographed against a dark background for definition of the fish's patterning, but in the aquarium, let there be light!

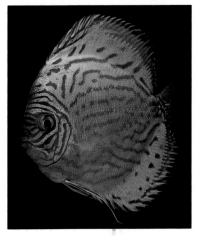

most important consideration in the aquarium because it affects so many functions. The health of plants is directly linked to the amount, and more importantly, the duration of the light they receive, for it provides the energy they need for photosynthesis. Fishes also require light; it is vital for their metabolism, and in many species it will determine their reproductive capacity. It will also affect their color as is easily appreciated if you consider the pallid fishes and plants that are native to low light habitats—such as cave fishes and plants denied light artificially. In such cases they exhibit little or no color. Discus are found in shadowy but clear waters where dappled sunlight plays all day.

There is no reason, however, to go to extremes with the lighting. For an aquarium with a depth of 20 inches, two side-by-side fluorescent tubes are satisfactory. With a 24-inch deep aquarium, a third fluorescent tube can be added. Warm-tone lights are preferred. The color of the light depends somewhat on the aquarium owner's taste. If you prefer more subdued light, which gives the fishes a reddish tint, you should use the familiar Gro-Lux tubes. If you prefer more natural light, however, then the use of warm-white tones or

These beautiful one-year-old brilliant turquoise Discus show their full color in the light of a warm-toned fluorescent bulb. Another kind of lighting might bring out more red in their pattern. It's amazing how different lighting affects how the eye perceives the colors of Discus.

special tubes, which are commercially available from various firms, are recommended. Your aquarium shop owner will be able to help you select suitable tubes.

The daily light period is 12 to 14 hours, and should be regulated with a timer for the benefit of both fish and plants. Plants can accommodate unnatural light conditions within reason as long as the duration of the light is correct. In any case, the light should be switched on a half-hour before the first feeding. In this way the fishes can adjust to the new day and are already alert and active.

If the aquarium is located in the living room, it will usually receive a corresponding amount of daylight. This can mean that the aquarium lighting will not have to be turned on until later in the day and can stay on longer in the evening. Aquaria that stand in the living room, however, should not be exposed to direct sunlight, since otherwise they will be overgrown with algae and big problems will result. Algae problems scarcely ever turn up with artificial lighting, especially in soft-water conditions.

Discus tanks can also be open on top. This provides the opportunity for large Amazon swordplants to grow out of the aquarium and even to flower. The disadvantage of having an aquarium open on

Aquarium lighting has literally come out of the dark ages in recent years. The manufacturers have responded to our desire for special effects and applications with a wide variety of lighting options. Your pet shop dealer will help you review the available choices.

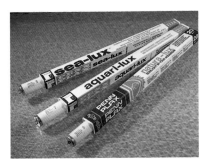

top, however, is the high rate of evaporation, because even in the Discus show tank a minimum temperature of 82°F. must be maintained. A temperature of 84°F. is even better. At this high water temperature a large amount of aquarium water evaporates. Under certain circumstances the water must be replenished several times a week. A disadvantage of replenishment of water, however, is the enrichment with additional minerals. The water used to top up the tank enriches the aquarium water with more and more mineral salts. For larger open aquaria it is advisable to use a small complete desalting installation or a reverse-osmosis device. In this way you can produce the required amount of desalted fresh water, which you then use to fill the tank. Because this desalted water contains scarcely any minerals, the mineral content of the aquarium no longer rises as much.

Lighting Alternatives

While fluorescent tube lights are excellent, if they have a drawback it is that their diffused light does not penetrate to the lower levels of very deep tanks, nor are they very good for creating variable lighting effects. For those wanting especially bright light, other lamps are available. Metal-

Deep tanks require that special consideration be given to lighting to ensure that the plants at the bottom receive the light they need for growth and health.

halide lamps (quartz-halogen) produce very bright light but are expensive. They will need to be suspended about 12 inches above the aquarium, which should have no canopy or hood.

Mercury vapor lamps are somewhat less expensive than the metal-halides, yet they generate considerable brightness, especially when housed in a suitable reflector. Again, they are suspended above an open-top aquarium.

Sodium vapor lamps are available, but since they have a strong bias toward the red end of the spectrum their application in aquatics is limited unless they are combined with blue-biased lighting.

There are many varieties of spotlights that can be used over aquaria, and by fitting them with various shades or reflectors, one can direct beams of light to specific parts of the aquarium to create stunning light-and-dark areas.

HOUSEKEEPING IN THE AQUARIUM

The true master and expert is revealed in the restraint shown in stocking the aquarium. A restricted biologic circulation prevails in the aquarium, which is easily disturbed by overpopulation with fishes. Because it is a question of a Discus show tank, the stocking with beautiful Discus is of course the main objective. At least 15

The type of light you use will have a strong impact on the red coloration of your fish.

gallons of aquarium capacity is the standard for a full-grown Discus. A 90-gallon aquarium could be stocked with six Discus. Small Discus are not suitable for Discus show tanks. To rear these small Discus successfully demands close attention, regular feeding several times a day, and several partial water changes a week. Therefore, it is recommended to acquire at least half-grown Discus, or one-year old or full-grown fish.

Quarantine

Before new fishes are introduced into an existing aquarium, they must go through a suitable quarantine period. With Discus this means a quarantine of at least two to four weeks to make sure the fish are healthy. Only then may they be transferred to the show tank. On the whole it is advisable to introduce as few new fishes into the established aquarium as possible. It is better to determine at the start which fishes will be stocked and to introduce them together within a short period of time.

Water Changes

There are many devices on the market to make your water changing chores easier. The only advice is that you find a system that you are comfortable with and keep up with those water changes! Discus are particularly

Young Discus are best kept in a tank proportionate to their size for proper growth. Keep the show tank for the adults.

contented and grow better when a partial water change is carried out at least once a week. In a show tank the partial water change

is somewhat more problematic under certain circumstances, because the aquarium is of course located in the living room. This is no excuse for neglecting it, however, and you should get used to changing 10 to 20 percent of the aquarium water once a week. Food remains lying on the bottom are a problem for the water quality of an aquarium. In smaller show tanks, in particular, you must make sure that these food remains are siphoned off without fail.

Only careful attention to water quality and good rearing practices will allow a fish such as this outstanding red-spotted green Discus to reach its full potential.

Water for Discus

Now that we know the water conditions that are preferred by Discus, how do we achieve this special brew that will keep these wonderful fish in top condition?

Some Discus fanciers are lucky enough to live in areas where the water is naturally soft and acid and requires no modification. This is all too often not the case, however, and the water is more suited for rift lake cichlids or livebearers, i.e. very hard and very alkaline. There are solutions to this problem.

Good water quality plays a large role in the ability of your Discus to reproduce.

HARDNESS AND PH

Hardness is the way of expressing the amount of carbonates, bicarbonates, sulfates, and other salts dissolved in water, with calcium and magnesium being of primary concern. Hardness is expressed on the German scale as degrees of hardness (DH) which is a measurement of one part of calcium carbonate dissolved in 100,000 parts of water. Soft water usually has a DH of less than 3; medium water is about 6 DH; hard water is anything 12 DH or above.

Hardness of the aquarium water plays a

There is nothing like a large tank for putting good size on adult fish.

subordinate role in the show tank. After all, the object here is the successful keeping, not the successful breeding, of Discus. Therefore, the water can by all means be medium-hard, which increases the stability of the pH. On the whole, hardness is not nearly as important to the well-being of Discus as it is to their breeding. Why? Because with increasing water hardness the osmotic pressure of the water also rises and Discus eggs can survive in this water only conditionally. All the same, good breeding successes occur time and again in furnished show tanks with medium-hard water. Apparently the biological stability of the aquarium system has a positive effect on development. The pH is far more important than hardness in keeping healthy Discus. The pH in the aquarium must never be allowed to fall below 4.5. A sudden drop in pH in a short time can have particularly catastrophic results. The Discus will suffer injuries to the mucous membranes or develop white deposits on the eyes, or both. Once an eye is damaged, the injury is permanent and lowers the value of this fish.

Once you have adjusted the water to the desired pH, it is kept fairly stable by the substrate and the aquatic plants. There are many products available that will lower and raise the pH of your water. When testing for pH, aerate the sample before testing and you will get more accurate results from your test kit. The ideal pH for Discus is above 4.5 and below 7.0. The backwaters of the Amazon where Discus are found in abundance regularly test at between 5.0 and 6.0. If all other conditions in the aquarium are ideal, your Discus will still remain vital and healthy even at the upper value of pH 7.0.

ION EXCHANGERS

Ion exchangers are used to lower the hardness of the water by exchanging the salts in the water for neutral compounds.

Beads of synthetic resin, upon which the ions are deposited rather loosely, are used in ion exchange. These ions can easily be exchanged for other ions. The synthetic resin beads look something like sand and for this reason are best placed in a plastic tube in which the reaction with water can take place. Various plastic tube systems of this kind are commercially available.

REVERSE OSMOSIS

Another way to reduce water hardness for Discus is a process called reverse osmosis. Very simply, in reverse osmosis the water is "squeezed" through a fine membrane which "catches" the mineral salts and other impurities and renders the water essentially pure and free of minerals. Not only does reverse osmosis remove the minerals from the water, it removes heavy metals, organic contaminants, phosphates and nitrates, chlorine, and chloramine.

FILTRATION ALTERNATIVES

Filtration is life itself in the closed system of the aquarium. The filter is the true life support system. Without adequate filtration, in addition to regular water changes, your fish have no chance of *ever* reaching their full potential. Hygiene is

Ion exchange is one way of reducing the hardness of your water for optimal hatch rates of Discus eggs. This is just one of many styles and even though the outward appearance may differ from unit to unit, the operating principle remains the same.

utmost in any aquarium, but most particularly in the Discus aquarium. Discus have evolved to live in water that contains virtually no ammonia and very, very few of the bacteria that are present even in our tap water. To bring this fact home to you, tap water contains fewer than 100 germs/ml, but the Amazon contains only about 5 germs/ml. Sure, there are (few) places where the water quality is ideal right from the tap and large water changes can be performed daily, but this is not a practical solution for most of us; we must rely on the efficient filtration of the aquarium. Unfortunately, our tap water is not always satisfactory and sensitive fishes react in very negative ways to impure water. Even traces of pesticides or nitrate can cause problems in the aquarium hobby. Thus, a fairly large partial water change can under certain circumstances cause more problems than it solves. This makes an efficient and well-functioning filter all the more important.

Discus fanciers as a rule use two different kinds of aquaria. The first is the so-called breeding tank, which usually hold 30 to 50 gallons of water, and the second category includes the keeping and rearing aquaria, which usually have a capacity of 60 to 100 gallons of water. Therefore, different kinds of filter systems are required.

Mechanical Filtration
This is true filtration

Reverse osmosis is the water softener of choice for many aquarists. Again, there are many styles available on the market and it remains for you to choose the one that suits your needs best.

in that the water is passed through a filter medium that captures the particles of debris. The success of such filters is dependent upon the gauge of the filter medium—the finer this is, the greater its effect. Typical media are plastic strainers, nylon floss, sponge cartridges, and gravel, but any inert substance can be used that will trap particles.

Chemical Filtration

Dissolved gases and chemicals will pass straight through a mechanical filter. To remove these, substances are used that will react with such chemicals and render them harmless. The most common is activated charcoal and it will absorb many toxins, such as certain heavy metals and ammonia. You must remember that a chemical filter has only done its job once the media has actually been removed from the aquarium and cleaned; until then the chemical remains a hazard. Once the media has absorbed chemicals to its saturation point then it will cease to be a chemical filter and may release the chemicals back into the water to compound the situation, so it is essential that the media be removed and cleaned on a regular basis. Most chemical filters do perform a mechanical role for they will also trap larger particles of debris, and are often

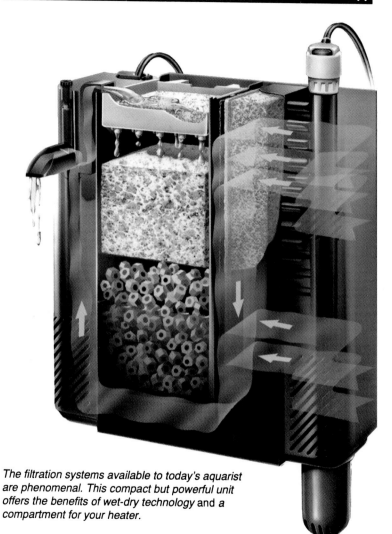

The filtration systems available to today's aquarist are phenomenal. This compact but powerful unit offers the benefits of wet-dry technology and a compartment for your heater.

used in conjunction with mechanical filters.

Biological Filtration

Bacteria (*Nitrosomas*) in the filter medium are always a prerequisite for a properly functioning filter. The hobbyist must recognize that the filter medium does not clean the water and decompose toxins, but rather the bacteria perform this function. The biological filtration performed by these bacteria is critical for the prevention of high ammonia, nitrate, and nitrite levels in the

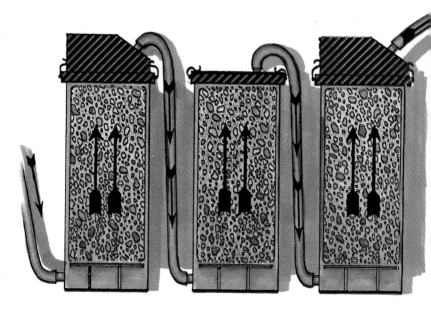

Canister filters can be "ganged" for extra filtration.

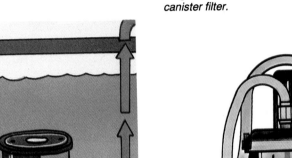

Diagram of the water flow through a canister filter.

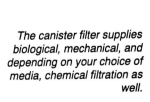

The canister filter supplies biological, mechanical, and depending on your choice of media, chemical filtration as well.

Young Discus of Schmidt-Focke checkerboard X Manacapuru parentage.

Eight canister filters! This is a serious filtration setup.

aquarium—the Nitrogen Cycle. Once this is understood, it makes absolutely no sense to clean the filter in such a way that the entire filter substrate is changed or scalded with boiling water. This suddenly removes all beneficial bacteria and the fresh filter medium cannot assume the function of cleaning the water in the aquarium because it is completely inert. Such a mishandled aquarium could even "lose its balance." It takes several days or even weeks for new bacteria to become re-established in thoroughly cleaned filters. Only then will the filter be biologically active again. For this reason the filter medium should only be rinsed briefly in

Professional Discus breeders use a lot of PVC pipe, hosing, bare tanks, and mega-filtration!

A popular and convenient outside power filter model.

An internal power filter that uses an interesting design to facilitate bacterial activity for biological filtration.

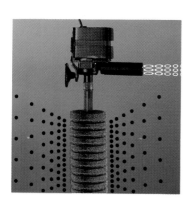

You can perk up your filtration with a sponge filter that attaches to a powerhead.

A sponge filter can be attached to the inlet tube of your power filter to act as a prefilter. This method also permits you to continue using your power filter while there are fry in the tank.

Pads for power filters are very convenient to use and provide good surface area for biological filtration.

lukewarm water. This is particularly true of filter systems equipped with sponge.

Most filters are used primarily to encourage the Nitrogen Cycle to function. The media provide a home for the beneficial bacteria to colonize. The most obvious medium is the gravel substrate, but there are many other possibilities, including the media in most mechanical filters.

The surface of the filter media is ideal for colonization by these beneficial bacteria and usually contains a ready source of food for the bacteria in the form of trapped organic matter. One of the more recent mediums is sintered glass that looks somewhat like a small airstone. It is claimed to be so efficient that water changes are reduced purely to that of replacing water lost in surface evaporation. Biological filters must of course have a good air supply and they do take some months to build up the effective colony size. They are easily destroyed by medicines added to the aquarium, so you must always be careful on this account—some medications claim not to harm such colonies.

If the bacterial colony is destroyed by over-zealous cleaning with hot water or if the power is off for some hours the water will turn sour and give the owner the impression that the problem is lack of oxygen, as the signs are

Give your power filter a real power boost by adding a sponge filter to the inlet pipe.

much the same—the fish gasp at the surface.

It is possible to purchase bacterial cultures from aquarium stores and these will speed up the formation of a colony. When an aquarium is first set up there will be no colony— which is why newcomers often experience problems when they put the fishes in before the aquarium has been given a maturation period for plants and nitrifying bacteria to establish themselves.

Vegetative Filtration

Plants in an aquarium assist in cleansing and they serve as

biological and chemical filters. In the old days of the hobby, before sophisticated filters became available and any filtration at all was only for the enlightened, fish often did well in heavily planted, lightly stocked aquaria. Many fishes do not feel secure unless they are in a well-planted tank and many owners feel they are missing out on some of the beauty of the aquarium unless they can also have an assortment of beautiful plants. If you wish to fully benefit from auxiliary vegetative filtration then it is a matter of simply passing the aquarium water through another heavily planted aquarium where algae and plants flourish.

Flow Rate

Flow rate is given in gallons-per-hour. As a general guide the complete aquarium water volume should pass through the filter twice in every hour—thus you simply double the tank capacity to establish the necessary flow rate. It should be noted, however, that power filter manufacturers usually quote the free-flow water rate, that is, how much the pump will turn over without any obstruction. Once the filter media is placed into the system, the flow rate will drop considerably and some

Facing page: Beauty aside, plants enhance your water quality by assisting in the removal of nitrate from the aquarium.

compensation should be made for the reduction.

Prefilters

Filter floss can be used as a prefilter in many filters. The visible, coarse particles of dirt are collected in the prefilter. Fine particles of dirt reach the lower layers of the filter and are decomposed there by bacteria. These floss prefilters can of course be rinsed out weekly or discarded.

Sponge Filters

Smaller filters have proven effective for breeding tanks. The water turnover should not be too fast and the flow should not be too strong in the breeding tank. If these aquaria are filtered individually, the use of a foam or sponge filter is recommended. These sponge filters are equipped with one or two sponge cartridges and are driven simply with an air pump.

The sponge filter is often overlooked, but is in reality extremely effective, particularly when raising fry. The surface of the sponge is an ideal medium for the nitrifying bacteria, collects particulate matter, and is host to rotifers that are nutritious food for fry and adult fishes. It is amazing to see just how quickly a cloudy aquarium is cleared when a mature sponge filter is introduced, and how clear it stays.

These sponge-cartridge filters can be operated for a very long time. It is only necessary to remove the sponges from time to time and to rinse them briefly with lukewarm water. Then the filter is fully operational again.

Sponge filtration can be supplemented with an additional power filter. At the moment I combine sponge filters with small outside filters. These recently introduced small outside filters are driven by a pump requiring only five watts per hour, and thus are an affordable alternative. The outside-filter box is hung on the aquarium rim and with the aid of the built-in motor the water is sucked through the small, but effective filter chamber and then is pumped back into the aquarium. These

Most serious aquarists use the very simple sponge filters for their smaller tanks.

outside filters are equipped only with coarse sponge, so that the water can flow through unimpeded. Naturally, it is also possible to add small amounts of peat or activated carbon to these outside filters. In this way it is possible, for example, to change the pH of the water with the peat. By using activated carbon, any medications that may have been added to the water can be filtered out. If Discus larvae or tiny fry are present in the aquarium, the inlet should be closed off with a sponge plug. In this way the water can still be sucked out, but

A familiar sight to veteran hobbyists, the box filter is humble and inexpensive, and yet does a fantastic job of filtering your water.

not the fry. The combination of a somewhat faster flowing filter system with a slow-flowing sponge filter seems to me to be a good solution.

Box Filters

The simplest filters of all are the small box filters that are made of plastic and can be situated in the corner of an aquarium. A plastic tube leads from its base and an airstone is fitted into this. A suitable filter medium, such as floss, or floss and charcoal, is placed into the box, which has holes or slots through which water can flow. It is also helpful to place a layer of marbles in the bottom of the box. They will prevent the filter box from floating

Power filters provide excellent filtration and convenience, especially the models that permit you to customize your filtering media.

around and provide a suitable surface area for nitrifying bacteria.

Once the box is placed into the aquarium it fills with water, including the tube that opens at or just below the water surface. Once the air is switched on, it creates the upward current that draws water from the area around it, thus the debris carried into the filter collects in the box which can be regularly removed so that the filter medium can be replaced or cleaned. It is a mechanical filter and has moderate biological filtration properties.

While the box filter is one of the oldest, and to some the most humble

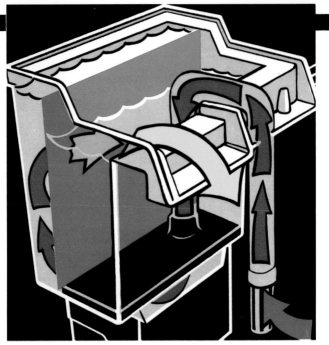

This diagram shows how the water moves through power filters. Just bear in mind that no matter how wonderful your filter, you still must perform regular water changes!

of the filters, it is still one of the most effective and ideal for those aquarists on a tight budget.

Power Filters

For smaller aquaria with a capacity of up to 60 gallons, the so-called power filter is very popular because of its efficiency, ease of maintenance, and reliability. It is simple to set up and simple to maintain. It creates both mechanical and biological filtration, and the addition of charcoal to the filter media provides the element of chemical filtration as well. Virtually every filter manufacturer offers his particular style and it remains only to select the one that suits your own taste and wallet.

The power filter hangs on the outside back or side of the aquarium and consists of a filter box and pump unit in one. The filter media is placed in the box and the water is drawn into the box through a tube inside the aquarium. The water then passes through the filter media and flows back, cleansed, into the aquarium.

Inside power filters are also suitable. The water is drawn into the filter chamber inside the aquarium and returned with the aid of the motor.

Canister Filters

Aquaria that are not overpopulated can be maintained well enough with an outside or canister filter. The canister filter is the workhorse of the aquarium. It seems a bit complex in the box, but once assembled, it is really

An internal canister filter will polish the water in a grow-out tank.

quite simple. The filter and mechanical parts are self-contained in the canister. Two hoses, one to withdraw water from the tank and one to return water to the tank, are attached to the canister. The canister is filled with layers of media that filter the water until it is crystal clear and biologically cleansed.

If there is enough room under the tank, then it may be a good idea to use this space and place the filter installation under the aquarium. This will make it possible to use a large canister filter with a pump head. Large canister filters can remain in service without cleaning for several months.

To simplify cleaning and backwashing, equip the line connections with the quick-release couplings that are available for the hoses at nominal cost.

Large canister filters are also available with built-in heating cables that eliminate the need for additional heaters.

Trickle Filters

The trickle, or wet-dry filter is very popular with Discus fanciers at the moment. Initially developed for marine hobbyists, the trickle filter has found a strong niche with the keepers of delicate freshwater fishes as well. These trickle filters are slow biological filters with an aquarium overflow and are very effective. A biological filter works *better* at higher pH values of about neutral, but is still quite efficient at the lower pH values preferred for Discus. The trickle filters must never be equipped with too fine a filter media because with the long standing times the waste particles decompose very quickly and foul the water. Special filter media for trickle filters are available on the market.

Central Filtration

Discus breeders frequently connect all of their breeding tanks in series and serve them from a central filter. The central filter is a multi-chambered filter with a prefilter and several filter chambers containing different filter media. These multi-chambered filters are correspondingly large in size. The size of the central filter for breeding tanks should amount to at least 20 percent of the quantity of water to be filtered. All of the breeding tanks are connected to this filter by a system of pipes. Holes are bored in the rear glass of the breeding tanks and an overflow pipe is installed. All of the overflow pipes then meet in a waste pipe, which runs to the multi-chambered filter. In this way, all of the water collected from the breeding tanks can be conducted into the prefilter chamber of the large filter. The water to be filtered then flows through several filter chambers and is collected in a clear chamber. Located in this clear chamber is a powerful pump, which conducts the clean water above the level of the breeding tanks. Located there is another system of pipes, with a branch for each breeding tank. Each of these branches from the main pipe is equipped with a faucet. This makes it easy to regulate the amount of water that runs back into each breeding tank. As the clean water runs back into the tank, the same amount of water to be cleaned will overflow into the waste pipe. In this way the circulation of the system is completely closed. Because of the high water temperature in the breeding aquaria, it should be kept in mind that a lot of water will evaporate. Therefore, it is necessary to regularly check the water level in the filter.

The main disadvantage to the system of central filtration is contagious fish diseases. Thus, it goes without saying that only healthy fishes may be introduced into a closed aquarium system of this kind. A quarantine period of at least four weeks must be observed.

Larger rearing or keeping tanks can also be connected together to a filter installation with a multi-chambered filter. Nonetheless, here the problem of the required quarantine and possible outbreaks of disease can often be a

Central filtration is desirable when there are a large number of tanks to filter.

real nuisance. It is better and more advantageous to equip each individual rearing or keeping tank with its own filtration system.

Filter Chambers

The filtration system you choose for your Discus show tank also depends in part on the configuration of the aquarium. If the aquarium is built into a cabinet, there is sometimes enough room to install a filter chamber next to the aquarium. This separate filter chamber could be integrated into the aquarium, but it seems better to install a separate, small filter-tank alongside. This

*Above: Each of these tanks boasts a gravel chamber for filtration. **Facing page:** The typical undergravel filter is a very simple piece of equipment with no moving parts to break.*

filter is divided into several chambers by vertical panes of glass. In this way the filter chambers can be filled with a variety of filter media, such as filter floss, ceramic tubules, gravel, or activated carbon. A pump is located in the last chamber, which returns the filtered water back to the aquarium. If this filter is of suitable size, the time between servicing certainly could amount to several months or even a year. In this case, however, a prefilter chamber equipped with filter floss is required. This prefilter chamber must be cleaned of gross waste once a week.

When using an undergravel filter, the gravel actually serves as part of the filter.

Undergravel Filter

The undergravel filter relies primarily on bacterial action for its efficiency and there is an element of mechanical filtration as well when the debris is trapped in the gravel. The undergravel filter uses a plate, usually plastic, that is raised about $\frac{1}{2}$-inch above the bottom glass of the aquarium. The gravel covering the filter and the space beneath the plate is home to the nitrifying bacteria that make this a very

Powerheads are very useful. They can be used to power an undergravel filter or a sponge filter. Some are equipped with containers for carbon or other media.

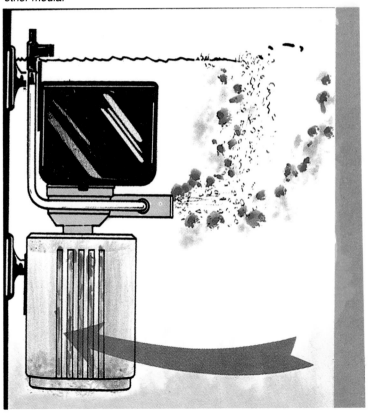

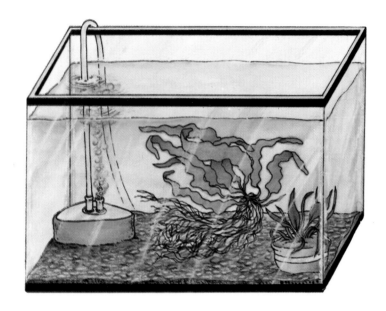

As long as there is adequate heat, very good fish can be raised in this simple setup. The sponge filter will certainly keep the water clean as long as the fish are not crowded or overfed.

effective biological filter. There are tubes, usually two, that are connected to an air source that draws the water through the gravel and under the filter plate where the bacteria do their job. I do not recommend undergravel filters for use with Discus because of the risks associated with power failure. Should the power be off for a short period of time the undergravel filter would quickly become anaerobic and deadly.

AERATION

The addition of extra air into an aquarium by mechanical means is termed *aeration*, and it provides many important advantages. If the air is released just above the substrate then it will attract water molecules and the air/water mixture, being lighter than water, will rise to the surface. In so doing it creates a current, thus causing circulation of the water. Equally important is the fact that during this same turnover, the carbon dioxide dissolved in the water is also released at the water's surface. An excess of carbon dioxide is just as dangerous as a shortage of oxygen. In an aquarium that is supersaturated with

Diatom filters do a remarkable job of clearing small particulate material from the water. They will even remove many disease organisms, such as protozoans. The water is filtered through diatomaceous earth, hence the name diatom filter.

oxygen, the fishes can still suffocate if the water contains too much carbon dioxide or other poisonous gas. The fishes' blood cannot rid itself of carbon dioxide quickly and therefore is unable to pick up the life-giving oxygen.

The bubbles produced when air is pumped into an aquarium contribute very little oxygen. It is the fact that they take de-oxygenated water to the surface that actually increases the overall oxygen content in the aquarium.

If the bubble size is small, and if a curtain of bubbles is produced by the airstone, then this will add some oxygen, which will be released when the bubbles burst. Not only do the air bubbles take poorly oxygenated water to the surface, but they also contribute in another way. When the bubbles burst at the surface they agitate the water, thus increasing the surface area, which allows for more oxygen to dissolve into the water than would be the case if the surface was undisturbed. With maximization of oxygen content, more fishes can be housed in an aerated tank than in the same tank that is not aerated. Aeration also aids in the removal of toxic gases.

The beneficial nitrifying bacteria that

Facing Page: Your sponge filter will not only clean your water, but seems to be a favored spawning site as well. What does this fish know that we don't?

convert dangerous nitrites to nitrates need a good supply of oxygen, so again aeration will have a positive effect on the aquarium's ability to remove harmful toxins.

Aeration will, of course, also reduce the risk of the water forming stratified layers, which would be the case if the water was still. It thus provides for more even distribution of heat throughout the aquarium.

The amount of oxygen in the aquarium will vary with the temperature, as well as other factors, and since Discus require fairly high temperatures it is a good idea to keep an eye on the oxygen content of the water. The higher the temperature is, the lower the oxygen content. You can test the water for its oxygen content by the use of a kit available from pet shops. By recording readings taken at various times, a picture can be built up of how things change over a period of time.

Airstones
The normal way in which air is introduced to an aquarium is via an airstone attached by a length of plastic tubing that is connected to an air pump. An airstone can be any porous material, such as felt, stone, or wood; usually the molded stones are used. It may be a small cube or a long rectangular diffuser. The amount of air released can vary,

not only by the pressure pumped in, but by the size of the airstone. It is usually placed near the back of the aquarium, often concealed behind a rock. By featuring two or more long airstones you can create a wall or curtain of air bubbles, which can look quite attractive.

While it is possible to keep Discus with no accessories other than a heater, you would need to have a lot of water and plants, very few fish, and perform enormous water changes. For most of us, this is not practical and we prefer to have more fish and less work. Choose your equipment carefully and you too can keep healthy Discus in abundance.

This "Royal Blue" is a first generation offspring of the classic "Haraldi" Discus from Rio Manacapuru in Brazil. The fish is chocolate brown with wavy blue stripes on the body and a dark band on the anal and dorsal fins.

Stocking Your Show Tank

SELECTING YOUR DISCUS

The mind boggles at the abundance and varieties of Discus offered by breeders today. It is not so long ago that a Discus fancier was overjoyed to acquire a plain brown Discus. The old-timers are full of stories of Discus fanciers waiting at the docks for shipments of Discus from Brazil. In fact, it is not so long ago that the only Discus available were delicate, wild-caught fish, but it is from this wild-caught stock that the pioneers of Discus breeding developed the blood lines that have given us the kaleidoscope of Discus varieties available today.

The first thing you should do when you are looking for your Discus stock is to locate a reliable dealer or breeder. This is a person who knows Discus and will willingly answer your questions about the fish. If possible, examine his tanks. They should be clean and not overcrowded. The fish you buy should preferably be of good, known parentage.

The Discus you select

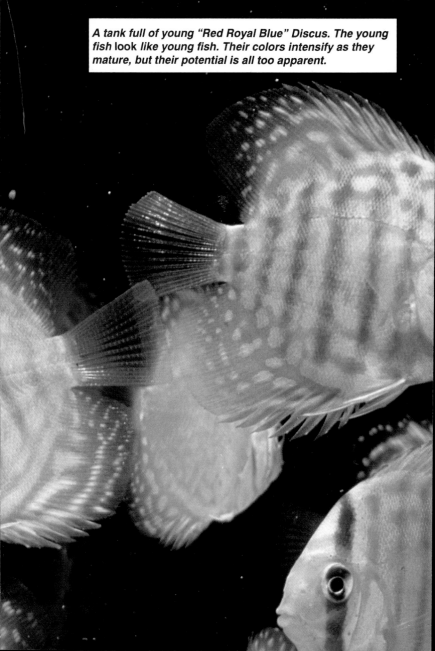

A tank full of young "Red Royal Blue" Discus. The young fish look like young fish. Their colors intensify as they mature, but their potential is all too apparent.

A wild-caught brown Discus. This fish shows a lot of the desirable red color.

should act like a healthy fish. Healthy fish are not shy, nor do they cower in the corner of the aquarium. They are not flighty nor easily spooked. They are curious and inquisitive. Often shyness is a symptom of disease. A healthy fish swims and eats like a healthy fish. It is confident and majestic in bearing.

The fins are upright and fully spread, not clamped or tattered.

The Discus you select should be the proper shape. That is, as close to round as you can imagine a fish to be. Young Discus, of course, like gangly teenagers, have not yet achieved this roundness, but are more elliptical. There are high-bodied Discus available and they are not the classic, rounded shape, but rather have been bred for body height. Otherwise, you

These fine fish represent the ideal. They took first place at a highly competitive international fish show.

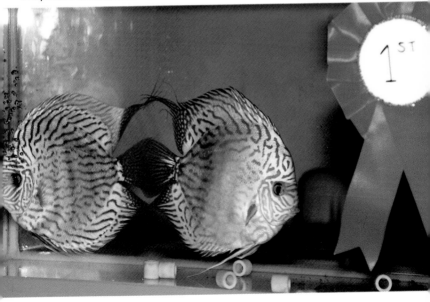

If you have the opportunity, examine the fish out of the water for defects.

mouth to the caudal fin.

There are desirable traits in Discus, and there are desirable traits. A universally desirable trait of Discus is the "tomato-red eye." The eye of a good Discus is perfectly round, bright and clear, and the black pupil is surrounded by a tomato-red iris. Again, proportion is important. An overly large eye for the fish is an indication of stunted growth.

Look for deformities. The gill covers should be perfect and flat. The fins should also be perfect, not tattered, short, crinkled, or in any way deformed. The

are still looking for a discoid-shaped fish. The fish should have a high, sharply sloping forehead. The body outline should be even. The distance between the dorsal and ventral fins should be equal to or greater than the distance from the

Facing page: The average size of an adult Discus is about 5.5 to 6 inches (without the tail). This fine specimen is enormous, full-bodied and a credit to his keeper.

One of the outstanding features of the Discus is the tomato-red eye.

The size of the eye should be in perfect proportion to the body of the fish.

skin should be perfect and without scrapes, abrasions, bloody spots, or missing scales. There should be no parasites! The abdomen should be prominent and the body thick and full. The head is small compared to the rest of the body.

Color and pattern are

Desirable red turquoise with great form.

a matter of personal preference. The color of your choice should be strong and clear. A darkened fish is often unwell or frightened. Look for unusual and attractive patterns.

ACCLIMATING NEW FISH

When you finally bring your new Discus home to the beautiful aquarium that is set up and waiting for them, consider that they have been through a lot. Not only have they been netted, bagged, and jostled, but they have probably been in the dark, and are running out of air fast. To unceremoniously dump them into a strange tank would be a little unfair, to say the least. There is a simple procedure that will enhance their chances of making the transition from dealer's tank to your beautifully furnished show tank with the least amount of trauma.

You will need a clean container large enough to hold the Discus and twice the volume of water they came home in. Install a gentle airstone in the container. Gently release the fish and the water into your container. Then, over the next hour or so, slowly add small amounts of water from your aquarium. This will dilute the dealer's water and gradually acclimate the fish to your water's values and temperature. Then you simply net the fish and

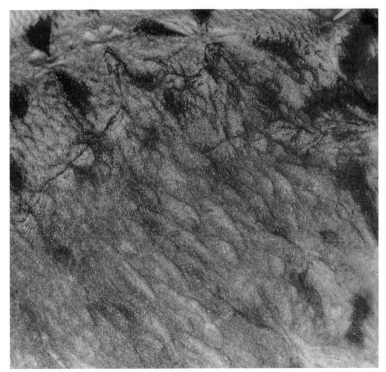

An unusual strain with textured, irregular scales, known as "Moonscape."

release it into its new home. Turn off the aquarium lights for an hour, but leave the room lights on so the fish are not completely in the dark in their new surroundings. Do not feed the fish until they are completely at home, usually one day at least.

COMPANIONS FOR DISCUS

Why would the Discus enthusiast bother to keep any other fishes? One good reason that comes to mind is the "dither fish" phenomenon. Highly intelligent fishes like Discus often make their decision to investigate strange waters only after they have seen other fishes swimming unmolested. If you have suitable dither fish you just may have calmer, more secure Discus. Another reason for having some other fishes is for the service they perform in keeping the aquarium neat and tidy. If you want the algae kept to a minimum automatically, then by all means you will want to keep some of the suckermouth catfishes. If you want the gravel kept clean of leftover food, you will opt for a few *Corydoras* sp. The third reason that comes to mind is simply that you *want* some variety and contrast.

Which fishes are suitable as tankmates for Discus cannot be answered all inclusively. The Discus must remain dominant in the show tank, so under no circumstances may active, larger fishes be introduced. Angelfish are not suitable because they crowd out the Discus at the feeding place. In the selection of the byfishes make sure that they also come from South America and occur in approximately the same biotope as the Discus.

It would seem that Discus and angelfish would live in harmony together, but this is simply not the case. Adult angels are very aggressive in their temperaments, feeding, and breeding habits especially when compared to Discus.

Catfishes

Peaceful catfishes are suitable as bottom fishes and while they should not be thought of as "scavengers," do in truth provide a pretty good vacuum service for the show tank.

The genus *Sturisoma* deserves special mention. *Sturisoma panamense* and *Sturisoma aureum* are ideal companion fishes for a Discus show tank and also for unfurnished keeping tanks. These graceful catfishes with their long barbels and fins are absolutely peaceful and dependably clean the aquarium of food remains. Numerous catfishes of the genus *Hypostomus* are now available on the market. Not only do these suckermouth-type catfishes provide additional interest to the aquarium, but they do a fantastic job of keeping algae off the inside surfaces of the aquarium. This translates into a little less maintenance on your part. These catfishes are very attractive and can only be described as peaceful as far as Discus are concerned. They do, however, tend to be a bit scrappy at times among their own kind. They can "dot the i" in a Discus show tank.

The Midget Sucker Catfish (*Otocinclus affinis*) is a great little algae-eater. In fact, practically all its waking hours are spent cleaning algae off every surface. Because they

While small plecos can be useful as algae controllers, avoid large ones that might disturb the Discus.

are only about two inches long, you might want to have a few if you expect them to do all the algae-removal. Their primary food is algae, so don't forget about them when the algae runs out. Some parboiled zucchini or spinach, or other veggies will help hold them over along with a share of the Discus' menu. Cory catfishes of all species (*Corydoras*) are wonderful in the Discus aquarium. These comical little fellows are very good-natured and hardy. They will use their sensitive barbels to snoop bits of food from the gravel and do a bang-up job of housekeeping.

Ancistrus sp. are special for their "bristle-noses." They have a number of bristles that cover the upper head and mouth areas and stand out in all directions. These bristles are exceptional tactile organs that allow the fish to feel its way around in the darkness to feel out whatever food is available. What a conversation piece! With an average adult size of about six inches, they are not likely to outgrow their allotted space in the community aquarium.

Schooling Fishes

South American tetras can be kept in

Facing page: Otocinclus affinis is a good choice for a Discus show tank.

schools with Discus. It is a beautiful sight in a show tank when a school of Cardinal Tetras makes its rounds. Schools of Black Neons or Neon Tetras provide attractive contrast.

Cardinal Tetras (*Paracheirodon axelrodi*) are the classic companions for Discus. They are so vivid and colorful when properly kept that some people keep schools numbering in the hundreds. Luckily, they require the exact same conditions as Discus for optimal health and beauty. For the best results with Cardinals, remember that they are schooling fish and should be kept with at least a dozen of their own kind.

Neon Tetras (*Paracheirodon innesi*) are very similar to Cardinal Tetras, but lack some of their extraordinary coloration. Otherwise, there is very little difference in keeping requirements, size, diet, or breeding habits.

Members of the genus *Hyphessobrycon* are star attractions in schools of six or twelve. They are absolutely peaceful and colorful to boot.

Tetras of the genus *Hemigrammus*, like the Glowlight, Garnet, Rosy, and Rummy-nose are perfectly suitable for your show tank.

The Harlequin (*Rasbora heteromorpha*) is a native of the Far East. If you are a stickler for an authentic Amazonian aquarium,

Corydoras *species are benign companions for Discus and certainly perform a useful service. They will ferret out morsels of food from the substrate.*

Paracheirodon axelrodi, *the cardinal tetra is the classic companion for Discus. These small, extremely colorful fish require the same soft, acid, and warm water as Discus.*

Harlequins will not be part of your picture, but if you want some lovely, gentle, schooling fish,

Cichlids

By virtue of being a Discus enthusiast, one is also a cichlid fan, for

Hyphessobrycon amandae.

you won't go far wrong with these little fellows. They make excellent companions for your Discus and thrive in the same conditions favored by Discus.

what else is a Discus? Other cichlids that are great for the Discus aquarium include Rams (*Microgeophagus ramirezi*), a gorgeous, peaceful, dwarf cichlid.

Above: Hemigrammus erythrozonus. **Below:** Hemigrammus rhodostomus.

Crenicara, Nannacara, and *Apistogramma* specie are all small and peaceful and absolutely authentic companions for Discus. They all uproot plants or rearrange the gravel to suit themselves. Any territorial behavior you might observe is a component of mating

Rasbora heteromorpha.

have identical keeping requirements and will only enhance your living picture.

The dwarf cichlids are unique among cichlids in that they are very peaceful and will not and not likely to damage any of their tankmates. For their peace of mind be sure the aquarium is equipped with some small caves they can call their own.

Hyphessobrycon bentosi.

THE PLANTS

The desirability of plants in the show tank can hardly be debated. The spectacle of a stand of healthy plants can only enhance the beauty of the aquarium, and we know that plants also contribute to the purity of the water as well.

After your show tank has been set up and all the equipment is operational, the first aquatic plants can be introduced. When choosing plants for the Discus aquarium be sure that the species can tolerate the elevated temperatures required by Discus. To plant the aquarium as authentically as possible, it is best to use only aquatic plants from South America.

Well suited, therefore, are the swordplants of the family *Echinodorus*, many of which are native to South America. A Discus aquarium should not be crammed with plants, as the Discus need ample swimming space, so be sure to choose plants that won't take over the tank. Discus

Apistogramma cacatuoides.

Above: Microgeophagus ramirezi. *Below:* Crenicara filamentosa.

also get used to hiding behind dense plantings, which gives the observer little opportunity to see these beautiful fishes. It is *Echinodorus tenellus*. This grasslike, delicate swordplant is the ideal foreground plant. Recommended for the

Imagine a school of your fantasy Discus in this gorgeous tank.

is better to choose a few robust solitary plants and to space them well apart. Low-growing *Echinodorus* swordplants can be placed in the foreground. The best suited dwarf swordplant middle of the aquarium is *Echinodorus parviflorus*, the Black Amazon Swordplant. A valuable new plant for the middle of the aquarium is another subspecies of *Echinodorus parviflorus*,

Echinodorus parviflorus.

namely *Echinodorus parviflorus* "Tropica." It grows only 5 to 6 inches high and forms a compact rosette. Tall-growing *Echinodorus* species, are particularly attractive as specimen plants in larger aquaria.

Echinodorus are usually marsh plants that grow on the banks of still as well as moving waters. During flood periods the whole plant is submersed and often grows very different kinds of leaves than when it grows above the water line. Only a few of the species are actually aquatic and grow permanently under water, e.g. *E. amazonicus*, *E. parviflorus*.

All the species of *Echinodorus* are quite easy to grow and are not sensitive to external conditions. They require a good depth of sand and either neutral, slightly acid to slightly alkaline water which should be soft to medium-hard. The only really critical requirement is that they must have sufficient light.

The following are some of the *Echinodorus* species that are suitable for your Discus show tank. The Small-leaved Amazon Swordplant (*E.*

amazonicus) has long, lanceolate, plentiful leaves that meet at the base of the plant. It is a good specimen plant at about 15 inches in height, and under the proper conditions will produce a floral stalk from which new plants arise. *Echinodorus paniculatus* (Amazon

Echinodorus tenellus *in the foreground.*

Anubias barteri.

Swordplant) is somewhat larger (about 20 inches) than *E. amazonicus*, but similar in appearance and keeping requirements. Both species will, when allowed to grow out of the water, produce sturdy flower stalks that can grow over 20 inches. The dwarf *Echinodorus*, *E. grisebachii* (Chain Swordplant) and the forementioned *E. tenellus* (Pygmy Chain Swordplant), are excellent foreground plants that will quickly form a carpet of short, thick foliage.

The Water Aspidistras, *Anubias* sp, while natives of tropical Africa are exclusive (and expensive) enough to merit inclusion in the

Discus aquarium. They are ideally suited to the conditions we are offering the Discus and boast several very attractive species.

Alternanthera sessilis varieties are from southern Brazil and with their reddish leaves will give some color relief in the aquarium. They are easy to cultivate and care for and prefer an established aquarium with older water.

Cryptocoryne species are beautiful and popular, but there are consistent reports of poor results with them in the Discus aquarium. The fact that they are all natives of Southeast Asia should put up a red flag to the Discus enthusiast. They are not appropriate for the show tank. They do not

Echinodorus paniculatus.

do well in the high water temperatures favored by Discus and they are low-light plants that cannot stand competition from other plants. They do acidify the water, which is probably why so many Discus keepers have tried them, but the drawbacks are many and they do require more knowledge and care than any of the many recommended plants. Save your money.

The above-mentioned plants are only a few of the available and desirable plants that will do well in your Discus aquarium. There are many good reference books that will help you make further selections. Whatever you do, avoid the common, coarse, and plain ugly. They have no place in the Discus aquarium. There are many plants sold for the aquarium and one can only wonder: Why? Make sure the plants you buy are actually aquatic plants. Some retailers offer hardy terrestrial plants for aquarium use. They will last for a while, but there is no hope for them. They will never grow or thrive and the only end result is rot. Rotting leaves do not contribute to water quality and they clog filters. If a plant has brittle stems that are easily broken, avoid it. Likewise avoid plants that litter. There is no room in a Discus show tank for plants that make a mess.

Before you introduce

Alternanthera sessilis *var.* lilacina.

Wattley Coerulean Discus.

Plants for aquarium use are often grown hydroponically in great numbers ensuring optimal quality.

your plants to the aquarium be sure to check for snails. No offense intended to those snail lovers out there, but snails are unwelcome visitors in a planted show tank. They will munch their way through your beautiful and expensive greenery and they are a distraction. Besides, they are very prolific and while one or ten might not be a problem today, you will be very vexed by the thousands of their offspring marching through your tank in a few months. To cleanse your new plants of snails and their eggs, dip the plants in a solution of alum and water for a few minutes and rinse well before adding the plants to your tank.

FERTILIZER

The use of fertilizer is often recommended, but the Discus fancier must be somewhat careful here, for large amounts of fertilizers can cause problems for Discus. Therefore, it is recommended not to use fertilizers at first but to wait to see how the plants grow. The fish themselves will in time add a certain amount of "fertilizer" to the water which will enrich the substrate for the plants. In a new

Many aquarium plants, like this Echinodorus horemani, *will flower when kept under optimal conditions.*

aquarium that is essentially sterile as far as the plants are concerned, you may want to purchase potted plants. The little pots contain a planting medium and a small amount of slow-release fertilizer that will ensure your plants are getting the nutrients they need until the aquarium is well established.

The use of carbon-dioxide fertilization seems to be more suitable than organic

Echinodorus cordifolius *with inflorescence.*

fertilizers in the Discus aquarium. If excellent growth of aquatic plants is important to you, you may want to investigate a carbon-dioxide fertilization system for your aquarium. There are many complete systems commercially available. It goes without saying that the pH of the aquarium water must be checked regularly when carbon-dioxide fertilization is used. Very soft aquarium water is prone to large fluctuations in pH. Discus, however, do not tolerate these fluctuations particularly well.

If all your efforts at attaining the planted aquarium of your dreams fail, there is always the ubiquitous, hardy, plastic plant.

The sight of large, healthy Discus eating from the hand is enough to melt the heart of any Discus enthusiast.

Foods and Feeding

One of the greatest pleasures of keeping fish is feeding them, and Discus are no disappointment in this arena. Healthy Discus have healthy appetites. They are quite happy to eat just as often as you are willing to feed them. When you see a Discus that isn't feeding (the kinds of foods it has previously relished), most likely it is sick or harassed.

Discus are cichlids and thus are primarily carnivorous. In its Amazonian homeland the Discus feeds on small freshwater crustaceans. In captivity it is possible to acclimate the Discus to almost all kinds of substitute foods. Because Discus have already been bred over many generations, they have largely lost the dietary habits of their wild conspecifics.

As a school fish, the young Discus can become accustomed to any sort of suitable food. If the attentive breeder regularly offers many different kinds of foods to his young fish, he will always have an easy time of it with the growing fish.

If your adult Discus have been spoiled and will not readily accept a new good food when offered, don't be surprised. It is unrealistic to toss an unfamiliar food into the tank and expect adult Discus go to crazy for it. The hobbyist may have to siphon off the food after a half-hour for several days because the fishes have not eaten it. After a few days, however, success will have been achieved. It is particularly easy to accustom fishes to new food when at least one fish in the aquarium readily eats it. Out of jealousy the other fishes will acquire the taste on their own.

Frequent large feedings are unnecessary; in fact, fishes in the aquarium are usually overfed. In nature, they nibble almost constantly so they are getting very small quantities of food all day long. This is not usually practical for those of us who must spend time away from our aquaria during the day, but several small feedings will net us healthier fish.

Adult Discus do best with four measured food portions a day. On the other hand, fry must be reared quickly with no disruptions in growth. Heavier feeding is required here, but the old precept, "feed frequently but sparingly," still applies. You can safely feed your fry up to ten times a day, but measure the portions so precisely that all of the food is consumed within a few minutes. And remember that regular partial water changes go hand in hand with the heavy

Yes, Discus will and should eat flake food. One technique often used to put weight on fish fast is to offer a normal feeding of flake first when the fish are hungry, and then some irresistible food like bloodworms shortly after. This entices the fish to eat his fill.

Pellet food is quite acceptable for Discus as long as the pellets are small enough for the Discus to eat comfortably.

feeding of fry.

Dry food in the form of flakes or tablets can be on the menu of our Discus. A daily feeding plan for adult Discus could be as follows: flake food, heart, then whiteworms, and finally frozen *Artemia* are each offered in a separate feeding. This provides the fish with a balanced diet. If one or more of the foods are additionally fortified with vitamins, deficiency diseases will be prevented.

LIVE FOODS

While Discus are not as fussy about their diets as their owners usually are, they do have some pretty definite needs as far as their menu is concerned. Live foods are necessary for the well-being of discus, and live brine shrimp (*Artemia salina*) are tops. Perhaps part of the reason Discus are so fond of brine shrimp is that they are a neat little mouthful and a bit of fun to chase as well. They don't move so fast as to be actual *work*, but they do move. Although live brine shrimp are first choice with any fish, for our convenience brine shrimp are also available in frozen and freeze-dried forms.

Brine shrimp eat algae. It is the algae that the shrimp eat that provides carotene in a form our Discus can utilize. Discus cannot metabolize carotene in it's original form, like carrots, but when they

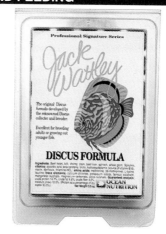

Nutritious Discus diets are available in convenient frozen form.

To enjoy the full color of your fish, be sure to offer some color-enhancing foods. There is nothing even remotely dishonest about feeding for color. In fact, it's good for your fish and poor color denotes a lack in some element of the diet.

eat the brine shrimp that have eaten the carotene, it greatly enhances their colors.

Midge larvae are the classic Discus food for half-grown and adult Discus. These are offered as white, red, and black midge larvae. Live midge larvae are not easy to obtain. All three kinds are available frozen on the market. As a freeze-dried product only red midge larvae are of importance. Red midge larvae certainly are not as valuable as black or white midge larvae from a nutritional and physiological point of view. Furthermore, midge larvae usually contain environmental pollutants. The presence of heavy metals in midge larvae

should not be underestimated. Bacteria and parasites can also be introduced into the aquarium with any live food. This is not a danger with freeze-dried midge larvae, but Discus are not fond of too small, freeze-dried midge larvae. A shortcoming of freeze-dried foods is that they always float at the surface and do not sink readily. The Discus, however, prefers to take its food from the bottom.

Whiteworms are another nutritious live food for Discus. These worms are a good food, but they are somewhat troublesome to rear. Whiteworms are reared in boxes; simple styrofoam boxes are ideal. The whiteworms

Foods like these tablets that stick to the glass are useful because you can see how much the fish are eating and there is less food lost to the filter and substrate.

are hard to separate from the soil in which they are reared. The following trick is useful. The clumps of soil containing whiteworms are put under a lamp—a desk lamp is suitable. The heat dries the clumps of soil and the whiteworms form into a ball in the center. As soon as the clump of soil falls apart, the pure, clean whiteworms can be collected. Whiteworms are highly prized as a conditioning food. The feeding of whiteworms once a day to pairs of Discus soon brings the female into spawning condition. Vitamin solutions can also be mixed in the whiteworms' food, thereby enriching them with vitamins.

Bloodworms are rich;

they should be fed only in small quantities as a treat. They should be rinsed often to make sure that the water they are being kept in is meticulously clean. Make sure also that there aren't any unwanted hitchhikers (leeches) in with the bloodworms. Tubificid worms are not recommended for Discus. They are so tainted with heavy metals that poisoning, gastritis, and enteritis can result. Unfortunately, this is also true of many red midge larvae, which are readily eaten by Discus. Filmy, thread-like droppings can be an indication of enteritis. If this is suspected, smaller portions of food must be offered. Midge

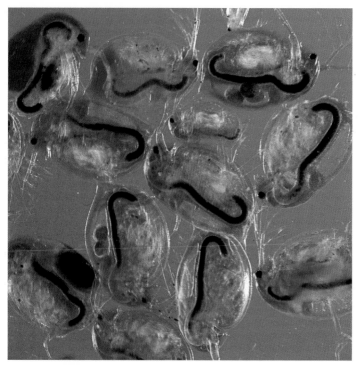

The live food menu is large and diverse. These daphnia are tasty little morsels for your Discus.

larvae should be taken off the menu. Only food of perfect quality may be offered.

Larger Discus will cheerfully devour baby guppies, but again, feeder fish are often infected with various diseases. Of course, if you were to raise them yourself under optimal conditions, they would be safe to feed to your Discus. We can never emphasize enough the value of feeding live foods to your aquarium fish. They are often thought of as the *haute cuisine* of the aquarium, but in truth they should really be considered the meat and potatoes. Live foods give your fish a zest for life that just can't be duplicated.

Earthworms are the finest food for fish.

They carry no diseases and are very clean. Leave them in a bit of shredded newspaper for a day and even the soil in their intestines will have been evacuated. Simply rinse and chop and you have very high-quality food that is full of vitamins.

There is tremendous variety on the live-food menu. Just imagine how many different kinds of insects and crustaceans there are in the world to get some idea of the kinds of live foods available. Just a few of the commonly used insects (and/or their larvae) include: Mosquito larvae, gnats, glassworms, vinegar eels, microworms, *Daphnia*, *Gammarus*, *Asellus*, and whiteworms. Many

Clockwise from top left: *Brine shrimp, blackworms, tubifex worms. Of the three live foods, brine shrimp are the only recommended foods for Discus; however, many people persist in the dangerous habit of feeding tubificids on the grounds that their fish like them.*

insects will send your fish into a feeding frenzy. Just make very sure that when you do feed the fish fresh insects that there is no possibility that they could have been contaminated with insecticides.

FROZEN FOODS

There are any number of frozen foods that your fish will take with relish: brine shrimp, bloodworms, krill, liver, beef and turkey heart, and spirulina are but a few. When using frozen foods you must rinse and thaw the food. Frozen *Artemia* especially are packaged in a briny soup that must be rinsed off. Place a portion of the frozen food in a fine net and rinse under the tap for a few moments. It will then be ready to feed to your Discus.

Discus also relish tiny bits of shrimp, clam, mussel, crab, and fish. A small piece of frozen minced cod will last a long time. It's fun to give your fish a variety of foods and they don't all have to come in a package. All it takes is a little imagination and your fish can have a different dinner every night of the week.

PREPARED FOODS

Discus breeders like to feed beef heart. Beef heart, however, sometimes has a bad reputation. Definite advantages are the ease of handling and ready availability of this food. One disadvantage is that the water is fouled

Left: Freeze-dried blackworms.

Right: Freeze-dried tubifex.
Below: There are many different prepared food formulas available for feeding your fish.

badly by the food remains. Overlooked remnants of beef heart soon start to decay. Therefore, when feeding beef heart, the hobbyist must be sure to siphon off excess food as soon as possible. Because of its coarse fibers and high collagen content, beef heart can cause constipation. Fine turkey heart is commercially available as well as beef heart and has become a favorite with Discus.

All fat and sinews must be removed from the beef heart. Then it is cut into cubes and shredded in a food processor. Whole pieces can also be frozen, then shredded with a grater as needed. Nut graters are ideal.

There are many prepared foods on the market and whether your Discus will accept them or not is something only you can know. There are specialized flakes, tablets, pellets, granules, freeze-dried foods, and on and on. Often the dried foods even come with a feeder to measure out the food and keep it in one area of the tank for easy clean-up of the leftovers.

FASTING

Just as it is healthful for most people to fast for a day, from time to time, it is also good for your fish. Fasting will give their digestive systems a rest and promote a good appetite the following day.

Bosmina *are small freshwater crustaceans that are suitable for growing Discus.*

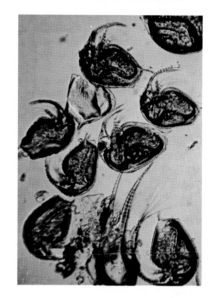

Bloodworms are often fed from a cone feeder so the fish don't have to chase them all over the tank with subsequent waste of the food.

VITAMINS

Feeding methods that fall outside the norm can surely be designated as progressive. Because the Discus is also somewhat outside the norm with respect to its feeding habits, methods will be presented here that bring amazing success. For example, the vitamin requirements of fishes, especially ornamental fishes, has not yet been sufficiently studied. This is also not surprising when we consider that the action of vitamins in the human body still leaves many unanswered questions. Vitamins A, D3, and E are very important for ornamental fishes. Determined by diet, vitamin deficiency—avitaminosis—can occur in Discus. Hypovitaminosis, that is, chronic vitamin deficiency, apparently can also occur, particularly in ornamental fishes. Vitamin A—retinol—occurs most abundantly in plants. It is better known as carotene. As carnivores, Discus logically are prone to vitamin A deficiency. With herbivores, most of the vitamin A that reaches the digestive tract is ingested in algae or diatoms. There it is taken up by the fish and converted. With carnivores, such as the Discus, this is not usually the case, except in small doses when the Discus eat the herbivore that ate the carotene.

Above: *An active whiteworm colony will produce ample worms to feed your fish.*
Below: Cyclops *nauplii add variety to the menu.*

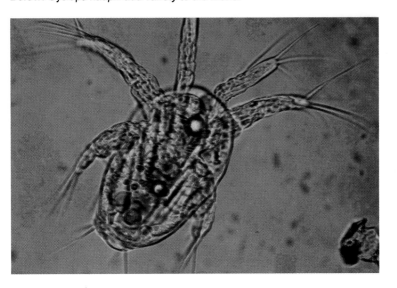

Vitamin A deficiency produces the following symptoms: poor growth and reduced food intake, fading of body ground color, reduction in color intensity, permanent damage to gill covers, and a reduction in liver mass.

Vitamin D is present only in small amounts in nature. Vitamin precursors, the provitamins, however, are present in abundance. The Discus must convert these precursors inside its body. How the fish meets its vitamin D requirement has not been studied. It is hard to say what symptoms of avitaminosis appear in vitamin D deficiency. Vitamin D deficiency in fishes usually means that there is a deficiency of vitamin D3. Because fishes store excess vitamin D3 in the liver, it is advisable to add vitamin D3 supplements to the food. When you buy frozen or prepared foods, take note of the vitamin and mineral supplements they contain. They should list the ingredients as well as the vitamins, minerals, protein, carbohydrate, and fat content. Discus, like any other living being, require a certain amount of the proper vitamins, minerals, and trace elements for health and reproduction.

Because disturbances in growth are frequent

Facing page: Grindal worm breeding setup.

Above: *Adult male chironomid midge.* ***Below:*** *Bloodworms are the larvae of the chironomid midge and not real worms at all.*

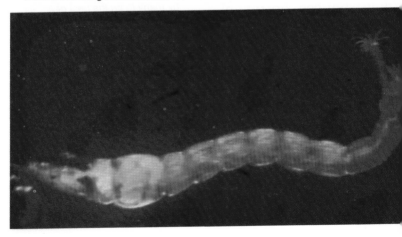

with Discus, close attention must be given to vitamin supplements. Metabolic disturbances lead to the loss of calcium from bone, which make them brittle, as well as softening of bone and gill-cover deformities. Gill-cover deformities are particularly frequent in young Discus. These damaged young fish are lost, because no one will be willing to buy them. Besides dietary disturbances, hormonal disruptions, hereditary deficiencies, and bacterial infections can also be responsible for gill-cover deformities. In any case, fry should receive vitamin supplements.

The one-sided first feeding of Discus with *Artemia* nauplii can be

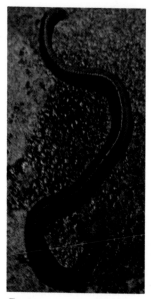

Earthworms are considered by many to be the best of all possible live foods for Discus.

responsible for disturbances in growth. The brine shrimp absolutely must be fortified with vitamins before they are fed to Discus. After only a few days the fry already take tablet food in pulverized form. As soon as the fry take food tablets stuck to the glass or on the bottom, feeding is no longer a problem.

If the parents are

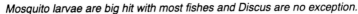

Mosquito larvae are big hit with most fishes and Discus are no exception.

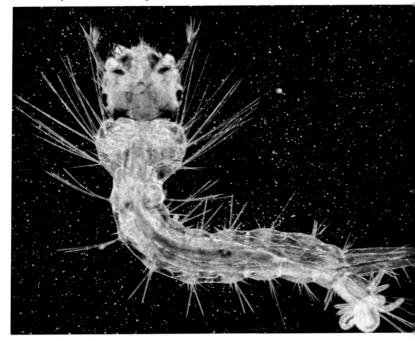

Top: Brine shrimp eggs are easy to hatch for feeding young Discus.
***Bottom right:** Brine shrimp, Artemia salina.*

doing a poor job of rearing—that is, they are fighting with each other and have to be separated—so that only one parent leads the fry—the breeder must offer supplemental food as soon as possible.

FOOD FOR FRY

One of the delightful things about Discus is that the parents feed the fry for the first few days. You don't have to worry about infusoria cultures or powdered fry foods that will foul the water in the rearing tank. While the fry are fed by their parents, they can still be seen to nibble at other foods in the aquarium. They will pick at the sponge filter for the rotifers living on the surface. Be prepared, however, and start your brine shrimp hatching right away because the babies will soon need to be fed and you will need to be ready.

Artemia nauplii are the first important food source. These tiny brine shrimp are reared in culture bottles. This is very easy. About one quart of water is put into an empty bottle, to which a heaping teaspoon of sea salt is added. Normal table salt would work as well. Next add one to two level teaspoons of brine shrimp eggs, add an airline for circulation, put it in a warm place— about 68 to 80°F—and wait for the eggs to hatch in about 24 to 30 hours. Light improves hatching results.

After hatching, the brine shrimp are siphoned off, sieved, and offered to the Discus fry. The Discus accept this food readily starting on the fifth day after they become free-swimming.

Under the watchful eyes of their doting parents, these Discus fry feed on the microscopic rotifers residing on a mature sponge filter.

The show tank can be used to "grow up" young Discus preliminary to breeding.

Breeding Discus

The family behavior of Discus has been a thrill and a joy to Discus fanciers ever since these fish were first bred in the home aquarium. The new parents, mother and father both, are closely followed by their newly free-swimming fry. The fry feed off their parents' bodies. Mother and father *both* "nurse" the young in the early days of life. Photos alone cannot do justice to the beauty of this behavior. To see a school of young Discus so close to their parents is a sight never to be forgotten.

Facing page: Over 250 baby Discus enjoy their first meal of brine shrimp.

THE RIGHT ENVIRONMENT

In this chapter useful tips will be provided from my experience. First we will turn our attention to the breeding tank. The ideal standing height for an aquarium for breeding Discus starts at three to four feet, measured from the bottom of the aquarium. Therefore, with an 18-inch-high aquarium, the height of the top rim would be 54 inches. I raise my breeding tanks 12 inches higher than that. From experience it can be said that the fish are not alarmed as readily at this height. This is connected with the angle of incidence of light. Discus kept in aquaria at leg height are always noticeably more timid. A frightened Discus naturally will not think about breeding. Sometimes fishes in sterile, unfurnished aquaria are so alarmed that they race into the sides of the tank and can even die from their injuries. This can be observed in fishes starting at three months of age.

The Discus recognizes its keeper and is used to his or her calm movements in front of the aquarium. When strangers visit the aquarium, quiet is the first commandment. Healthy fishes, which respond readily to food, will inquisitively come up to the glass when a visitor appears. During feeding they will literally eat out of your hand. Light also plays a role. Because a breeding tank contains no plants, the light can safely be somewhat dimmer than in a planted aquarium. Choose a warm-tone fluorescent tube, such as Gro-lux. When the fish lead fry, or from the time of egglaying on, you should leave a small light on all night. Fasten a lamp socket over the aquarium and use a night light, which will provide plenty of light. Discus sleep. When you turn on the light in the morning, you will see the fishes resting motionless on the bottom. If you fed them right away, the fishes would not take any of the food. The uneaten food could foul

Part of the author's breeding setup.

The proud parents guard their wrigglers.

the water. Wait at least 15, better yet 30, minutes before you feed your fishes. Only after this waiting period will the fishes be active and accept the food readily. When you notice that the fishes are ready to spawn, turn off the filter until the eggs are laid, but no longer than one hour. Strong current disturbs the fishes during spawning and, despite differences of opinion, can cause the eggs not to be fertilized properly. In the wild Discus spawn in standing water.

HOUSING FOR BREEDERS

Most Discus fanciers do not get by with a single aquarium for Discus. The goal of their hobby is to breed these

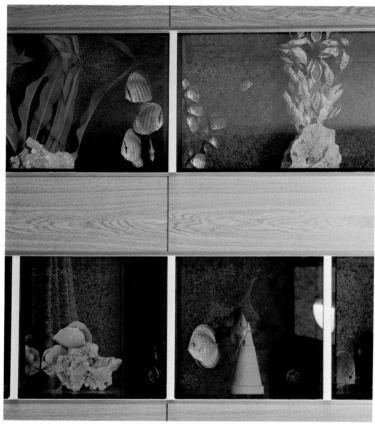

A selection of Discus of different sizes, kept by size and variety.

splendid fishes too, so a Discus breeding installation soon follows. What options do you have for reaching your goal? There actually are two good methods, each with advantages. The first is the separate tank installation wherein each tank is treated as a separate unit, each with its own equipment. The second treatment is where there are many tanks hooked up to a central filtration unit. Both types of breeding installations have their

A well-maintained Discus breeding station in Hong Kong.

pros and cons. The one you choose will depend on your tastes and your pocketbook, for the second version is somewhat more expensive at the outset, but depending upon the ultimate size of your breeding operation, may actually be less expensive in the long run.

Individual Filter Option

Several aquaria are set up on a shelf. The ideal dimensions for Discus breeding tanks are 20 to 30 inches long, 20 inches wide, and 20 inches high. Small deviations are of course acceptable. Because this kind of aquarium is never filled completely, it has a capacity of about 30 gallons, which is quite adequate for two adult fish.

What is the best way to filter these aquaria? Inside filters combined with sponge cartridges have proved effective for this purpose. A good high-output air pump will power the sponge filters and inside filters for four or five breeding tanks. The small, motor-driven outside power filters are also available on the market. These power filters are hung outside and are driven by a powerful yet efficient motor. If the Discus lead fry, the opening of the inlet tube must be reduced in size sufficiently with a covering so that the fry cannot be drawn into the filter. Small sponge plugs are the best

An entire aisle is devoted to Discus in this large pet shop.

protective covering.

That should be a sufficient number of tanks to start. The advantage of these separate breeding tanks is obvious. Each aquarium can be tended separately. Special water can be put in each aquarium. Extra medicines can be used in each aquarium and so forth. A cardboard screen should always be inserted between each aquarium, so that the fishes are not always in sight of one another. The rearing drive of notorious egg-eaters can be stimulated if an "enemy" in the form of another Discus lurks in a neighboring aquarium. The fishes should not be disturbed during the spawning act, so at this time the screen between the aquaria is quite an asset.

Common Filter Option

The second option is to set up a closed installation. The aquaria stand side by side, but are connected to a common filter installation. All manner of plastic (PVC) pipes, as well as suction discs, angles, T-branches, couplings, and much more besides, are commercially available. You can build a filter installation with this plastic pipe. Holes of suitable size are bored in the rear glass of the aquaria by a glazier. The overflow pipe with a right-angle bend is inserted in this hole. For safety, the bend outside of the water has a hole bored in the top, to prevent all of the water from draining out. In the event of a power failure, air enters the outflow pipe and the water no longer flows into the filter. The

Very young Discus feed from the sponge filter.

outflow is collected under the aquarium in pipes and from there flows through a coarse filter and into the filter tank. A fairly large kitchen colander, in which two thin layers of foam are inserted, can serve as a coarse filter. Water from all of the aquaria is collected in the first filter chamber. This is the best place to filter with floss. In the second chamber the water flows over gravel and in the third over small ceramic tubules. The pump, which returns the water to the aquaria, is in the last clear-water chamber. With these pumps the hobbyist can now profit from the ornamental pond boom. Recently clever pond pumps with plenty of power yet low wattage have appeared on the market. If one of these pumps is located about 30 inches below the aquaria in a filter chamber, it is possible to supply three or four aquaria, each with a capacity of 50 gallons. If the filter tank is at the same height as the aquaria, five or six aquaria can be served by this pump without problems. The filtered water flows through a tube from the pump back to a system of plastic pipe. This pipe is located above the aquaria. By means of a T-branch and a faucet, also of plastic, a line is

Facing page: These are not show tanks, but the breeding tanks of a very serious Discus breeder.

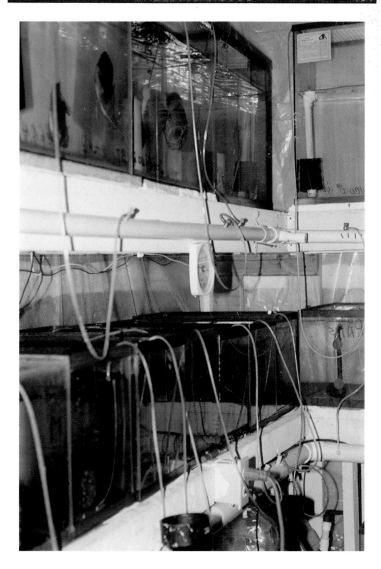

run to each aquarium. In this way each aquarium has its own inlet. The flow of water can be adjusted with the faucets so that about the same amount of filtered water runs back into each aquarium. In this manner the filter circuit is closed again.

These aquaria have the advantage of requiring comparatively little work. Supplying water is virtually maintenance-free. The disadvantage is that outbreaks of disease affect all of the aquaria, so for this reason it is advisable to combine these filter installations with an ultraviolet lamp. Bacteria are killed by ultraviolet light. Ultraviolet lamps have two water connections and are inserted in the water circulation after the filter, so that the filtered water is sterilized before it returns to the aquaria.

In aquaria serviced by these filter applications there is the danger, of course, that fry will be drawn into the filter. It goes without saying, therefore, that a safety device must be installed. For this purpose buy galvanized wire mesh of appropriate fineness in the hardware store. From it cut an appropriately sized rectangle. Bend this mesh into a circle,

Facing page: One of the parents tends eggs laid on PVC pipe.

closed in front, and insert it into the outflow opening. For this purpose, however, remove the long intake tube in the aquarium, so that the sieve sticks only in the hole bored in the rear glass. You can adjust the mesh size to the size of the fry in the tank.

THE SPAWNING SITE

Discus lay their eggs on smooth, vertical surfaces. Most fish breeders use a spawning cone. Fish will use the cone, but may at times choose a plant leaf, the side of the aquarium, or even the heater tube. However, clay vases are most commonly provided. Make sure the vases you buy are at least 8- to 10-inches high. If the

Wire mesh surrounds the filter intake pipe to protect the fry.

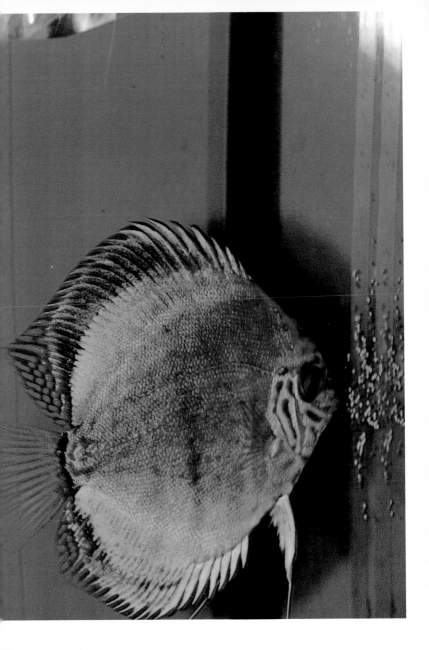

Your Discus will eat out of your hand when they trust you. This may take a few weeks, but it is proof positive that they approve of what you are feeding them, their tank conditions, and their owner.

vase wobbles or the bottom is not completely smooth, you should apply silicone cement around the entire bottom and then set the vase on a piece of newspaper. After the cement has dried you can remove the newspaper with water. The bottom of the vase is now soft and elastic and will stand steady.

SPAWNING STIMULI

A large water change is often just the stimulus needed for a pair of ready, but reluctant, breeders. Changing the water temperature by 4°F. along with the water change is another great way to trigger spawning. Changing the pH by one to two decimal places also helps. These adjustments mimic the effect a heavy rainfall in the Amazon which normally preceeds spawning.

As mentioned so often, live foods get fishes into spawning condition. Do not

Live foods equal healthy Discus and large spawns. These fish are enjoying whiteworms.

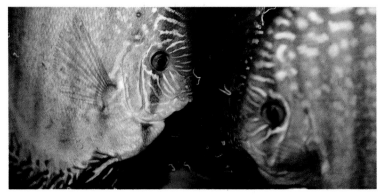

neglect this all-important element in Discus husbandry.

ABOUT FUNGUS

Many Discus breeders struggle with fungus attacks on the eggs. Aggressive fungicide treatment, however, can interfere with the production of the parents' essential food slime, so a different approach is necessary here. First, why are Discus eggs sometimes attacked by fungus? One reason is that the male may not have fertilized them. This, however, is rare. Another reason is that the sperm may not have had the opportunity to enter the egg. I have dealt with the problem of fungus infestation in many clutches of eggs. After the egg is laid, the sperm has only about two minutes to enter and fertilize the egg before the egg swells in the water and closes this entrance. If the egg is unfertilized it is attacked by fungus. In the wild, Discus lay their eggs in still water. This gives the sperm a chance to fertilize the eggs before being washed away. We should give the sperm an advantage in the aquarium by shutting off the aquarium filter during the spawning phase. This will give the sperm a better chance to fertilize many eggs. Consider that when the female lays a string of eggs and the male releases sperm, but it is swept away by the current produced by the

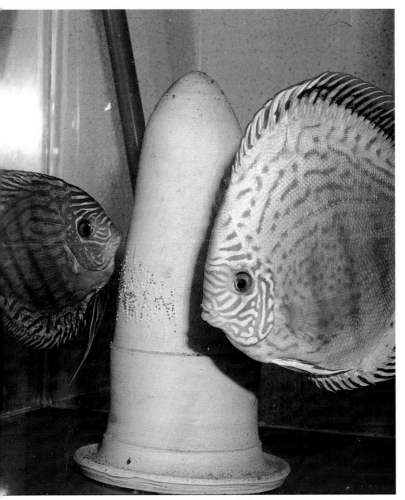

This female valiantly tends eggs that are already lost to fungus. She will tire of this as she realizes that these eggs will never hatch.

filter, that another two minutes may go by before the male returns. The result is that the egg opening of the first eggs will already have closed and the sperm will no longer be able to enter. Now I must turn to trout eggs. These have a hatching time of several weeks, which is dependent only on water temperature. The warmer the water, the faster the egg develops. The same is true of the Discus egg. At 82° F. the eggs require a development time of about 65 hours. At 88° F. the time decreases to about 55 hours. I have made tests with a water temperature of 77° F. and determined that the developmental period of the eggs was 72 hours. I was also able to discover that at high temperatures, above 84° F., the eggs were more likely to be attacked by fungus than at lower temperatures. This makes sense because fungus prefers higher temperatures and also reproduces faster under these conditions. Because fungus could be present anywhere in the tank, it must be killed.

The trout breeder handles this very simply with malachite green oxalate, which he uses once a week to bathe the fertilized eggs. In this way the trout eggs,

Facing page: The parents clean the pipe prior to laying their eggs.

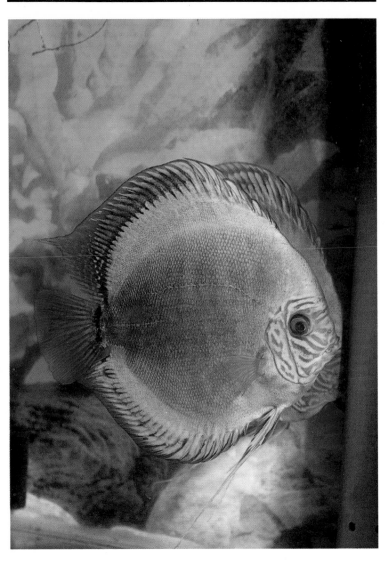

which, for example, have a hatching period of six weeks, are treated with malachite green oxalate six times during this period. The same procedure can be used with our Discus eggs. Working with rubber gloves, dissolve 1.5 grams of malachite green oxalate in 1 quart of water. Use 2 drops of this solution for each gallon of aquarium water in the breeding tank. Administer immediately following the end of the spawning phase. If after 12 to 18 hours either no eggs or only a few have been infested by fungus, then this malachite green treatment is finished. If a number of eggs are infested by fungus, however, repeat the treatment with half the previous dose. This second dose must, however, be administered no later than the end of the first or the start of the second day. Malachite green must not be added to the aquarium any later because it also disrupts the production of the skin slime. If you have the opportunity, filter the malachite green out of the aquarium through activated carbon when the fry are ready to hatch.

Another reason why Discus eggs are infested by fungus is too high a salt concentration in the water. The membrane of the Discus eggs can be compared to the leather covering of a football, except that the membrane is porous.

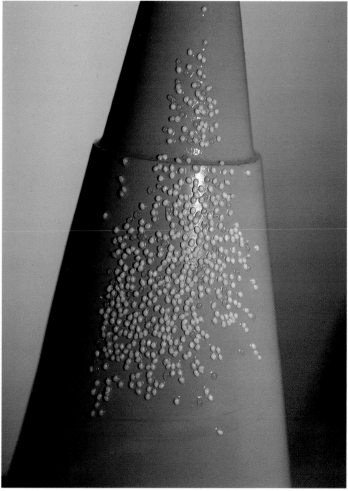

Unfertilized Discus eggs.

The bladder of the football, which holds air, corresponds to a thin layer of the egg membrane. This membrane is semi-permeable. High concentrations of salt cannot pass through the membrane. Small water molecules, on the other hand, can enter. Because this semi-permeable membrane prevents the large salt molecules in the cell from leaving the inside of the cell as they strive to balance the concentration of salts, water molecules enter the inside of the cell from the outside to lower the concentration of salts inside the cell.

This process continues until the pressure created inside the cell prevents more water molecules from entering. This pressure is osmotic pressure. When there are many dissolved salts in the water surrounding an egg, balancing the concentration outside the cell is achieved by drawing water from the egg. The egg shrivels and is no longer viable. The result can be clear eggs attached to the spawning cone, which do not continue to develop. On the other hand, the eggs are not always attacked by fungus; they have been damaged by the salty

Facing page: All your good feeding and keeping techniques will be for naught if you don't provide your breeders with the correct water conditions for the development and hatching of the eggs.

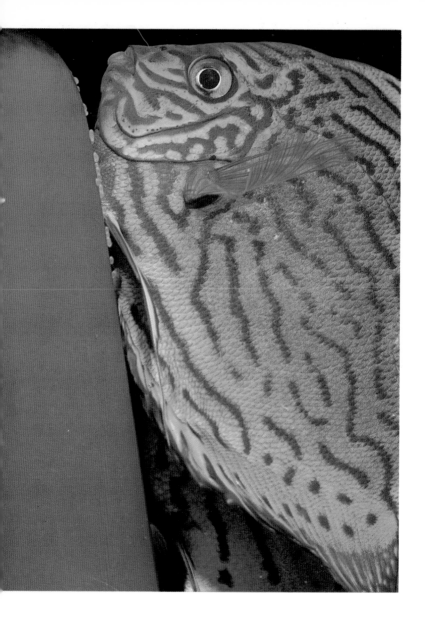

Wrigglers are "cemented" to the spawning site by a tiny thread attached to their heads.

water. The only remedy is partially or totally desalted water. Recently an increasing number of small reverse-osmosis installations have appeared on the market. By reverse osmosis almost all of the salt content is removed from the water and the water is also germ-free!

DEVELOPMENT OF THE BREEDING STOCK

The different Discus varieties can be crossed with one another. This means that by crossing different Discus lines, new lines with distinct characters are produced. By backcrossing with fish of the same line, inbreeding can be carried out, through which the desired traits can be stabilized. The goal of Discus breeding is to establish stocks with stable colors and forms, which produce the desired offspring over a long period of time. It would be ideal if two similar fish from two different stocks were crossed with each other. This line breeding, in which the characters of both original lines are retained, would be optimal. In pure inbreeding, setbacks occur frequently. In the selection of adult breeding stock, the breeder can easily evaluate the traits of the fish, since of course they are already present in their final form. Color, fins, and body form can be appraised.

Discus will eat their eggs and young if they feel they cannot care for them.

The male in the foreground shows
easily recognizable sexual differences,
such as the rounded forehead and
extended dorsal and anal fins.

Thus, whoever has the opportunity to buy three or four full-grown Discus each from two related or similar Discus stocks, has a good chance to put together one or two good pairs.

BREEDING STOCK

Discus breeding on a small scale is not particularly difficult and also does not raise any big genetic problems. The story is different, however, if you intend to breed a pure Discus line. There are so many different nuances of color in Discus today that it is scarcely possible to keep up with the names anymore. Because in principle all Discus can be crossed with one another, a color variety that is very interesting but is not purebred often results. If you want to make it your business to breed further such a color variety in good quantity, then you must be prepared to bear considerable expense, particularly because a lot of space is needed. A Discus line that pursues specific goals cannot be built up with only one or two aquaria.

In the breeding of Discus, line breeding and inbreeding must be distinguished.

Facing page: A group of baby turquoise Discus. At this size, the young can only hint at their potential.

Line Breeding

Line breeding serves to stabilize the homozygosity of the present stock, with special attention being given to desirable traits like color, body size, or behavior. These traits are the goal of breeding. In line breeding, two unrelated Discus lines are bred. Both lines should have approximately the same traits. Matings are made exclusively with fish of both lines. This means that the first parent will always come from the first breeding line and the second parent from the second breeding line. This prevents the deleterious effects of inbreeding.

Nonetheless, consistent line breeding with Discus requires a great deal of space. Imagine that the parents produce about 100 fry. These 100 fry must be reared to a minimum size of two to three inches, for only then can about 50 percent of these juveniles—those that meet your requirements—be sorted out. These 50 juveniles must then be reared to a minimum size of four to five inches. Only then can the beginnings of the coloration be optimally distinguished. Now the body form and any other desired traits

Facing page: The careful mother peeks out from behind the swordplant to monitor the whereabouts of her brood.

Yes, it takes a lot of space and work to successfully rear Discus in quantity.

can also be perceived. Consider, however, how much space is required to house 50 five-inch Discus. If the fish are too crowded they will not grow well. Simultaneously, 50 more Discus from the second breeding line must be reared. At a size of five inches and an age of about eight to ten months, another half to two-thirds of these fish can be selected out. The remaining Discus of each line are reared to full size to be used later for forming pairs. Thus it is necessary to rear at least 15 to 20 fish from each line. This takes a

The reward of seeing this kind of behavior far outweigh the work for the Discus breeder.

lot of space, intuition, and patience—not to mention the expense.

Only now is it possible to sort out the future breeding stock from these 30 to 40 large fish. The breeder will be very familiar with the fish he has reared, so he will be able to distinguish females from males with a fairly high degree of certainty and to put pairs together. Discus from two breeding lines mated in this fashion will produce fry that will inherit roughly stable traits.

Over several generations the colors can be intensified and stabilized through further selection. A Discus breeding stock built up and pursued consistently in this

manner will produce better fish from year to year.

Inbreeding

Another possibility in Discus breeding is offered by inbreeding. In inbreeding backcrosses are made between siblings or the parents, or both. This means that, for example, Discus from the F1 generation are backcrossed with their parents. This technique can achieve good results in a short time. Nonetheless, after four or five backcrosses setbacks in color and

Facing page: The young Discus feed primarily off the body of the parent, but will move up to the head region when the slime is gone from the flanks.

quality usually occur. The inbreeding of Discus is thus a way to stabilize particular traits quickly, but it is recommended to turn subsequently to line breeding.

PAIR BONDING

In the selection of the fish it should be kept in mind that it is possible to distinguish the sexes with Discus of the same brood. Females are usually somewhat smaller and more delicate in build than their brothers from the same brood. The tips of the fins also provide clues, because the fins of males taper more to a point, whereas those of females are more rounded at the tip. It would be ideal if eight large Discus were given the opportunity in a large aquarium to form pairs on their own. This also requires some patience, however, because the fish will not always cooperate immediately. Naturally, at least two spawning cones must be offered. The other option is to purchase at least ten fry from a brood and to rear them with a second group of similar fry from a second line. Clearly this takes more time. A Discus takes about a year to reach breeding age. From a school of twenty fry you can select the ten or twelve best after six months and rear them to maturity. It is preferable for the pairs to form on their own, because then it can be expected that they will also tolerate

A well-mated pair breeds often. These fish still have small fry feeding on their flanks and have another spawn ready to hatch.

each other during brood care. It is also possible simply to put pairs of adult Discus together in an aquarium. Whether it actually is a pair is not easy to determine. If the two fish tolerate each other, then it may have succeeded. This does not mean, however, that the pair will spawn together. With cichlids, and especially the Discus, the fish must be compatible. Merely confining them together achieves nothing.

I have made such attempts, in part involuntarily. When one male of a good pair died, I offered the good breeding female, which had repeatedly reared fry, three different males in succession, but none of them was accepted. No clutches were produced with these three males. Although the fish tolerated each other and were together for at least two months, no preparations for spawning occurred. Good breeding pairs have a harmonious "fish marriage." Because Discus do not spawn continuously the whole year, the breeder should have patience with his fish. He should leave the pair together, not tear them apart immediately, should a pair happen not to produce a clutch within a few weeks.

Facing page: The elongated fins and well-curved forehead seem to indicate that this beautiful solid blue turquoise fish is a male.

Ideally, Discus pairs should lead and tend the brood together. The fish alternate in feeding the fry with food slime. Occasionally, however, the parents fight over the fry. This is a difficult problem for the Discus breeder, because the entire brood can be put in peril. Removing one of the parents can be helpful, but can also have the opposite effect. Once the fry have reached the free-swimming stage, one parent can be taken out if they fight. It is more difficult if the parents fight over the clutch and eat the eggs. Some Discus are notorious egg eaters. Egg eating can subside, but these fish are usually permanently lost to breeding.

SEX DETERMINATION

This is certainly a question for which there is no pat answer. Unfortunately, the Discus has no reliable sex characters. Only during actual spawning is it possible to distinguish the sexes reliably on the basis of the form of the spawning papillae. The spawning papilla of the male Discus is shorter and tapers to a point, whereas the spawning papilla of the female is longer and blunter.

Experienced Discus breeders can distinguish the sexes of their fishes with a fair degree of certainty. Differentiation is also easier if fish from the same brood can be compared with one another. A popular sex

A rare event, the breeding of a pair of wild Heckel Discus.

character, which, however, is not absolutely reliable, is the more pronounced forehead of the male. If the fish has a more pronounced head area, maybe even a slight hump, it is usually called a male. When viewed from the front, the heads of males are broad and rounded to the outside. Females, when viewed from the front, have somewhat narrower heads. Fishes with protruding lips are often classified as males too. Elongated, straight pectoral fins could indicate a male. A somewhat more reliable character is the shape of the dorsal and ventral fins. The ends of these fins are rounded in females, whereas males have more tapered fins. The dorsal fin of males is also curved more on top, and the ventral fin is curved more to the bottom. The width of the tail fin also provides clues about sex. It is wider in males than in females.

The behavior of Discus in the aquarium can also provide clues about sex, but it is not true that the male is always the dominant fish in the aquarium. Females, even those that are smaller than the males present, can rule a Discus aquarium.

Females exhibit the dark vertical bars more often than do males. It is beneficial to observe the fish for a fairly long time and to study them closely. Then it is easier to make a sex determination on the basis of behavior and the external characters. This simplifies the selection and cohabitation of pairs. The behavior of the fish

This young turquoise Discus already shows a strong, red eye and proud, erect fins.

will then show whether or not the selection was correct.

A true "pair" will reveal itself by the mutual behavior of the fish. Now the attacks diminish perceptibly, the fish let each other feed without interruption—a very good sign—and ramming becomes less and less frequent. A dominant male will certainly stimulate the female to spawn and he will use force if necessary.

One of my Discus pairs repeatedly played out this splendid behavior. This pair had already reared many broods successfully and were very good parents. In the times between preparations for spawning, the female always had to suffer a great deal. The male always wanted to breed again as soon as possible, but the female was not yet able. The male rammed the female repeatedly, and continually drove her into a corner of the aquarium. At feeding time, however, the female was always allowed to take part and feed without disturbance. After that she had to return to her corner. After several weeks, however, when she had started to produce eggs again, the situation changed abruptly. She suddenly started to become an equal partner. In full splendor she hovered in the aquarium and allowed herself to be courted. Now there was absolutely no more ramming, only affectionate circling by the male. It did not take long before they spawned and cared tenderly and resolutely for the clutch and larvae.

Facing page: The female lays eggs in a string.

SUCCESSFUL DISCUS BREEDING

Once a pair has formed it will spawn. The colors of the fish change in the preliminary stage of spawning. The fish turn darker, more so in the rear part of the body. The last four vertical bars become clearly visible, whereas the transverse stripes in the front part of the body remain light. The stripes on the front part of the body disappear completely; only the stripe across the eye remains visible.

The fish stay at the spawning cone and start to tremble. This trembling is a twitching and shaking of the head. The next phase of spawning is cleaning. The fish vigorously suck

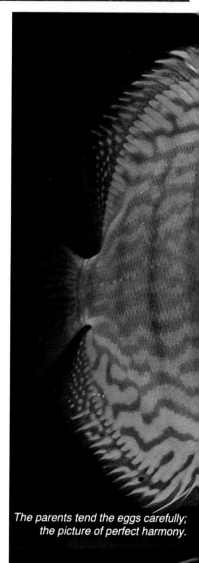

The parents tend the eggs carefully; the picture of perfect harmony.

dirt from the spawning cone. This intensive cleaning indicates that spawning is imminent. The female's spawning papilla or ovipositor now becomes visible. This broad ovipositor is clearly visible because it is about three to four millimeters long. The male's reproductive organ is shorter and slightly pointed. Soon

The pair has finally approved the cleanliness and suitability of the spawning site and will now commence spawning.

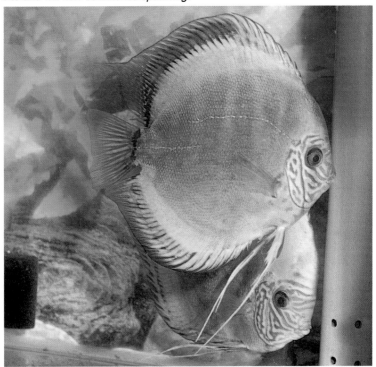

the female, in particular, starts to test for egg laying. She examines the spawning cone from bottom to top. Now it is hoped that the male will no longer allow himself to be warded off and will wait for the female to finish testing the cone, which can take up to an hour, and to begin laying eggs. The female swims up the spawning cone from below and lays a row of eggs. Now it is beneficial for the male immediately to swim after the female and fertilize these eggs. The female moves faster and faster and lays row after row of eggs. Medium-sized clutches have about 150 to 200 eggs. The

The fry will school until they are about six months of age; at that time they become more independent preparatory to mate selection and breeding.

largest clutches can have up to 500 eggs. The spawning process lasts about an hour. Watch the fish while they are spawning; they After the eggs are laid, the parents stay by the eggs and fan them with their pectoral fins. Harmonious pairs take turns. You can safely

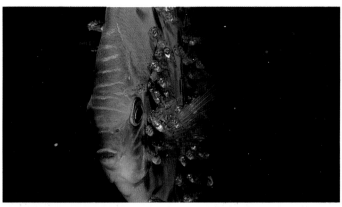

The aquarist is the third partner in the Discus parental group when he offers newly hatched brine shrimp to the hungry fry.

will paint a picture of perfect harmony. The sexes are easy to distinguish at this time, which could perhaps be very useful with a later change in mates. feed the fish during this phase, but you should not offer too much food, so that leftover food does not foul the water. The fish also do not eat as much now as usual.

Above: As the fry deplete the slime from the parent they have been feeding on... *Below:* ...they shift to the other parent without missing a beat.

It would be wrong, however, not to feed them during the entire breeding time.

Perfect Discus eggs are clear. The larvae hatch after a period of about 60 hours. This time can be reduced if the water is 86 to 90°F. The ideal breeding temperature is 84 to 88°F. After an additional 50 to 60 hours, the wriggling larvae start to become free-swimming. As the larvae hatch, they are sucked out by the adults and are usually moved next to the clutch. They hang there by a sticky thread. Larvae that become free-swimming prematurely are gathered up by the parents.

In so doing the parents seemingly "eat" the fry, but then swim back with the escapee to the brood and spit it back into its school of siblings. As soon as the fry are free-swimming it is important that they swim to the parents, for only then will breeding be successful. If they do not find the parents' skin slime, but swim around in the aquarium, they will soon perish. The reason for this aberrant behavior is unknown.

PARENTAL FEEDING

In the first four to five days, the fry feed exclusively on the parents' skin slime. The term "slime" is loose. Actually, the discus fry are ingesting the entire epidermis of the parent, except for the base

Many breeders use a mesh-type covering to protect the spawn from the chance that the parents will eat the eggs. This is said to encourage bonding so that inexperienced or flighty fish will properly tend the fry when the eggs hatch.

where it is formed. If you look closely, you can see how much energy the young fry expend tearing off the shreds of tissue. In the digestive tract of the fry, everything that they have eaten can be found more or less digested: epithelial cells, secretory cells, and the bacteria that live on the parents' skin. There is also evidence of other food, such as diatoms. Thus, the intestine, even at this early age, contains not only the parental slime, but food from the aquarium as well.

Parental feeding of the young is one of nature's inventions that considerably increases the success of a species. It increases the effectiveness of brood care, reduces losses among the young, and opens the way for smaller broods. This is evolution. However, there is a payback. This ability of Discus to provide food for their newborns has in a sense weakened them. Their skin is not the defensive weapon it is in less evolved fishes. Their fine skin is more easily damaged by bacteria and parasites. That is why Discus must be kept in a relatively germ-free, but not sterile aquarium. Bear in mind that along with the slime, the fry are subsisting on the bacteria that live on that tissue as well. This "Discus milk" is unique and incomparable food for their fry. If you think about the benefits to maternally nursed human infants, you will see that there are many benefits, especially for the immune system.The development of the slime is induced by hormones. The proper functioning of the hormonal system is strongly influenced by emotional health and diet. Stressed fish cannot produce the food their fry need. Think about this before you show your breeders to visitors!

Facing page: It is advisable to use a night light when your fish are leading young to prevent the fry from losing their parents in the dark.

CARING FOR THE FRY

Convincing Discus to breed is usually not a problem. A good pair does all the work; the eggs are laid, hatch, and soon grow into free-swimming fry. This is when the fish breeder's real work begins.

Feeding the Fry

Four or five days after the young become free-swimming, they are fed freshly hatched *Artemia* nauplii. Soon you can feed prepared foods for baby fishes, or *Moina* (miniature *Daphnia*), but continue to feed *Artemia* for a while. On this diet the fry will have reached the size of a quarter after four weeks. At this point they can be taken from the parents. After a total of six to eight weeks they will have reached the size of a half dollar and can already be sold.

Rearing the Fry

After three to four weeks the small Discus have reached a size of about one inch and must be separated from the parents. Now the real problem of Discus breeding begins, namely the successful rearing of the fry. An aquarium with ravenous little Discus is hard to care for. The water must be monitored constantly. Regular partial water changes, and this does

Facing page: This very interesting female was bred from wild brown and green parents. It is difficult to breed wild Discus, but the fresh, new blood is vital to ensure the vigor of the domestically produced fish.

not mean once a week, but daily, are necessary. Discus fry in this stage of development must be fed several times a day. First-rate rearing food is a prerequisite. A balanced combination of different foods is best. Essential—and this cannot be stressed often enough— are regular partial water changes. By means of the water changes, toxins, food remains, excreta from the fish, and so forth, are dependably removed. In the stronghold of mass

Facing page: When Discus are ready to spawn, even the presence of non-involved tankmates will not stop them. Unfortunately, the fry don't have much chance for survival when they arrive into a community setting. Even the Cardinal Tetras will prey upon the young.

Discus breeding in Southeast Asia, 70 to 80 percent of the water is changed daily in the rearing and breeding tanks. Because this would present us with a real energy problem, it is recommended to change about 10 to 20 percent of the aquarium water daily when fry are present. The rearing water does not have to be softened either. Medium-hard water can be used here without further ceremony. The

At two weeks of age these youngsters are already taking tablet food. The parents are depleted of slime and their skin coarse from nursing. They should have some rest and recreation to restore their energies before spawning again.

This is a very strong male with an excellent shape. A perfect mate for a high-class female.

This gorgeous red Tefé female could be used to highlight the red coloration in a breeding program. Although similar to the Alenguer reds, the Tefé fish are totally different. The Tefé green is well recognized, but the vivid red Tefé is true breeding and will pass the color on to her offspring.

A school of marvelous young red Discus.

Called "Blue Diamond," this variety is a dynamite turquoise strain. All the bars are missing and the youngsters show solid color at less than one inch in size.

A superb display of matched Discus. Each and every one of these fish looks healthy, well-fed, and eager. They are tame and hand feed readily. It should be no problem for these fish to pair off and produce thousands of tiny Discus identical to themselves.

Facing page: *A high-bodied turquoise Discus. This shape is highly favored in the Orient but has never really caught on in the West.*

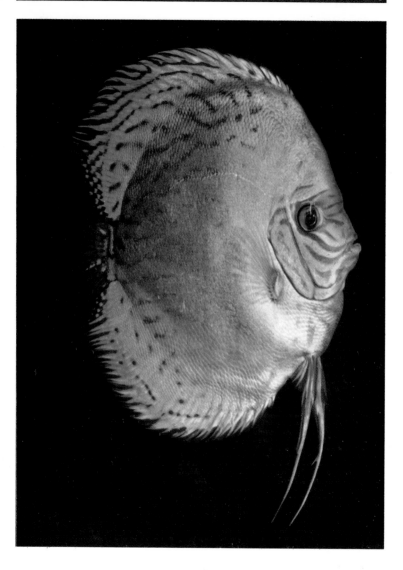

At about four months of age, this red turquoise shows tremendous promise with its deep, blood-red coloration.

pH can also safely rise to neutral levels. Many Discus breeders even claim that their fry grow much better in medium-hard than in soft water.

I can confirm this. I think that a higher mineral content of the water has a positive effect on the growth of the fish. It is also unnecessary to rear Discus fry at a temperature of 86°F. Temperatures of 81 to 82°F. are quite satisfactory for rearing

Cobalt blue male.

Pearl red Discus.

Facing page:
Heckel and blue Discus cross showing excellent colors.

purposes.

Fish take up minerals, trace elements, and vitamins not only in food, but also directly through contact with the medium of water. These substances are of great significance for satisfactory growth. In any case the offered foods should be fortified with trace elements and vitamins. Preparations with vitamin and mineral mixtures are commercially available. If you prepare your own food mixtures, in any event you should provide for an adequate supply of minerals and vitamins by administering preparations of this kind. An overdose is scarcely possible.

THE ALLURE OF DISCUS
by Dr. H.R. Axelrod and B. Degen
TFH TS-162, 10 x 14", 192 pages,
over 200 photos
The authors, one who has scoured
the Amazon in pursuit of discus, the
other a world-famous discus
breeder, have combined their
knowledge to produce this tribute to
the beauty of the discus.

THE ATLAS OF DISCUS OF THE WORLD
by Dr. H.R. Axelrod & B. Degen
TFH TS-164, 10 x 12", 368 pages,
over 350 photos
The combination of photos and hard
fact provided in this book make it
one of the most valuable discus
books ever produced. Especially
useful for distinguishing the many
beautiful discus varieties available.

DISCUS—A REFERENCE BOOK
by B. Degen
TFH TS-163, 8 ½ x 11", 128 pages,
132 photos
An invaluable reference that
provides vital information for anyone
keeping discus. Sections on care,
feeding, reproduction, health, and
more.

DISCUS FOR THE PERFECTIONIST
by J. Wattley
TFH TS-167, 9 x 12", 128 pages,
fully illustrated
The man who pioneered discus
breeding in the U.S., Jack Wattley,
has authored this book in unique
question and answer format. You
can compare and contrast the
knowledge of discus experts
gathered from around the world.

THE DEGEN BOOK OF DISCUS
by B. Degen
TFH TS-134, 8 ½ x 11", 160 pages,
360 photos
All the secrets of success with
discus are here. Bernd Degen loves
discus too much to jeopardize even
one by keeping his knowledge for
himself.

DR. SCHMIDT-FOCKE'S DISCUS BOOK
by Dr. E. Schmidt-Focke
TFH TS-135, 9 x 12", 128 pages,
180 photos
A bible from the German "Father of
Discus" Sage advice in
heartwarming anecdotal style.

DISCUS, HOW TO BREED THEM
by B. Degen
TFH TS-137, 8 ½ x 11", 160 pages,
100 photos
True facts about discus breeding
from the German master. Special
information not available anywhere
else.

Index

Page numbers in *Boldface type* indicate photos.

Acclimation, 120
Aeration, 105-109
Alternanthera sessilis, 141, **143**
Ancistrus, 126
Angelfish, 123
Anubias barteri, **140**
Apistogramma cacatuoides, **135**
Apistogramma, 133
Artemia salina, 154, **173**, 238
Background, 40
Beefheart, 162
Black water, 26
Bloodworms, **155**, 158, **170**
Breeding, 179-253
Brine shrimp, 154, **173**
Brine shrimp *nauplii,* 174, 238
Cardinal tetra, 128, **130**, 240
Catfish, 124
Central filtration, 97
Conductivity, 20, 25
Corydoras sp., 122
Crenicara filamentosa, 133, **136**
Cryptocoryne, *141*
Cyclops *nauplii,* **167**
Daphnia, 159
Discus,
    blue diamond, 247
    brilliant turquoise, **57**

    brown, **8**, **23**, **114**
    checkerboard X
      Manacanpuru, 80
    cobalt blue, **24**, **26**, **251**
    German "Wattley" type, **24**, **26**
    Heckel, **20**, **223**
    Heckel X blue, **253**
    moonscape, **121**
    red, **246**
    red pearl, **252**
    red dragon, **50**
    red royal blue, **113**
    red-spotted green, **67**
    red Tefé, **250**
    red turquoise, **42**, **119**, **250**
    royal blue, **110**
    turquoise, **7**, **221**, **225**
    turquoise high-body, **248**
    turquoise high-fin, **48**
    Wattley coerulean, **145**
Driftwood, 44
Earthworms, 160, **171**
Echinodorus, 135, 137
    amazonicus, 139
    cordifolius, 148
    grisebachii, 140
    horemani, 147
    tenellus, 137, **139**
    paniculatus, 139, **141**

parviflorus, 137
parviflorus "Tropica," 138
Feeding, 151-177, 238
Feeding, parental, 234-236
Fertilizer, 147
Filtration, 72-105, 186-194
Fungus, 198
Garnet tetra, 128
Glowlight tetra, 128
Grindal worms, **168**
Hardness, water, 25, 69-72, 250
Harlequin tetra, 128
Heating, 47-55
Hemigrammus erythrozonus, **132**
Hemigrammus sp., 128
Hyphessobyrcon bentosi, **134**
Hyphessobrycon sp., 128
Hypostomus, 124
Inbreeding, 206, 216
Ion exchange, 31, 69-72
Light, 42
Lighting, 55-62, 180
Line breeding, 212
Malachite green, 200
Microgeophagus ramirezi, 131, **136**
Midge, 158, **170**
Mosquito larvae, **172**
Nannacara, 133
Neon tetra, 128
Nitrogen Cycle, 82
Nitrosomonas, 78
Otocinclus affinis, 124

Pair bonding, 218
Paracheirodon axelrodi, 124, **130**
Paracheirodon innesi, 124
pH, 18, 21, 69-71, 250
Pleco, 125
Quarantine, 64
Ram, 131
Rasbora heteromorpha, 128, **133**
Reverse osmosis, 31, 72, 205
Rocks, 44
Rosy tetra, 128
Rummy-nose tetra, 128
Selection, 111-120
Snails, 146
Spawning cones, 194
Stocking levels, 62-64
Sturisoma spp., 124
Swordplant, Amazon, 139
    black Amazon, 137
    chain, 140
    dwarf Amazon, 137
    small-leaved Amazon, 139
Symphysodon discus discus, **17**
Substrate, 21, 42
Tank cover, 40
Temperature, 18, 47, 200, 251
Turkey heart, 165
Vitamins, 166, 252
Water Aspidistra, 140
Whiteworms, 156, **167**